WJEC
CBAC

WJEC GCSE

ENGLISH
LITERATURE

AIMING FOR A-A*

ROGER LANE

Great Clarendon Street, Oxford OX2 6DP

Oxford University Press is a department of the University of Oxford.
It furthers the University's objective of excellence in research,
scholarship, and education by publishing worldwide in

Oxford   New York

Auckland Cape Town Dar es Salaam Hong Kong Karachi
Kuala Lumpur Madrid Melbourne Mexico City Nairobi
New Delhi Shanghai Taipei Toronto

With offices in

Argentina Austria Brazil Chile Czech Republic France Greece
Guatemala Hungary Italy Japan Poland Portugal Singapore
South Korea Switzerland Thailand Turkey Ukraine Vietnam

Oxford is a registered trade mark of Oxford University Press
in the UK and in certain other countries

British Library Cataloguing in Publication Data

Data available

ISBN 978-0-19-913622-3

10 9 8 7 6 5 4 3 2 1

Printed in Great Britain by Bell and Bain Ltd., Glasgow

Author's acknowledgements

Grateful thanks to Wayne Powell, who understands people,
language and history; an unsung WJEC hero and a long-time
friend.
Thanks again to Nicola Dutton for her support and to Hayley
Cox and the team for all the professionalism in Oxford.

Contents

Introduction

SECTION 1: EXAMINED UNITS

SECTION 2: CONTROLLED ASSESSMENT

Features OF THIS BOOK

This book provides lots of useful features to help you consolidate your strengths and stretch your skills as you progress through your GCSE English Literature course. Here is a quick guide to what you can expect:

Sample student answers
Student answers give examples of top-grade writing.

Key words
Key word boxes provide definitions of important terms from the Assessment Objectives and marking criteria, to help you understand what you need to do to reach the top grades.

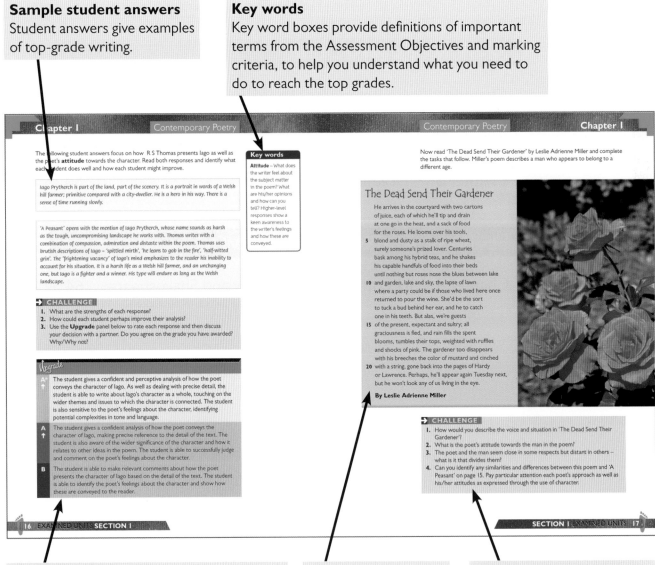

Chapter I — Contemporary Poetry

The following student answers focus on how R S Thomas presents Iago as well as the poet's **attitude** towards the character. Read both responses and identify what each student does well and how each student might improve.

Iago Prytherch is part of the land, part of the scenery. It is a portrait in words of a Welsh hill farmer; primitive compared with a city-dweller. He is a hero in his way. There is a sense of time running slowly.

'A Peasant' opens with the mention of Iago Prytherch, whose name sounds as harsh as the tough, uncompromising landscape he works with. Thomas writes with a combination of compassion, admiration and distaste within the poem. Thomas uses brutish descriptions of Iago - 'spittled mirth', 'he leans to gob in the fire', 'half-witted grin'. The 'frightening vacancy' of Iago's mind emphasizes to the reader his inability to account for his situation. It is a harsh life as a Welsh hill farmer, and an unchanging one, but Iago is a fighter and a winner. His type will endure as long as the Welsh landscape.

Key words

Attitude – What does the writer feel about the subject matter in the poem? What are his/her opinions and how can you tell? Higher-level responses show a keen awareness to the writer's feelings and how these are conveyed.

→ CHALLENGE
1. What are the strengths of each response?
2. How could each student perhaps improve their analysis?
3. Use the **Upgrade** panel below to rate each response and then discuss your decision with a partner. Do you agree on the grade you have awarded? Why/Why not?

Upgrade

A* — The student gives a confident and perceptive analysis of how the poet conveys the character of Iago. As well as dealing with precise detail, the student is able to write about Iago's character as a whole, touching on the wider themes and issues to which the character is connected. The student is also sensitive to the poet's feelings about the character, identifying potential complexities in tone and language.

A — The student gives a confident analysis of how the poet conveys the character of Iago, making precise reference to the detail of the text. The student is also aware of the wider significance of the character and how it relates to other ideas in the poem. The student is able to successfully judge and comment on the poet's feelings about the character.

B — The student is able to make relevant comments about how the poet presents the character of Iago based on the detail of the text. The student is able to identify the poet's feelings about the character and show how these are conveyed to the reader.

16 EXAMINED UNITS SECTION I

Contemporary Poetry — Chapter I

Now read 'The Dead Send Their Gardener' by Leslie Adrienne Miller and complete the tasks that follow. Miller's poem describes a man who appears to belong to a different age.

The Dead Send Their Gardener

He arrives in the courtyard with two cartons
of juice, each of which he'll tip and drain
at one go in the heat, and a sack of food
for the roses. He looms over his tools,
5   blond and dusty as a stalk of ripe wheat,
surely someone's prized lover. Centuries
bask among his hybrid teas, and he shakes
his capable handfuls of food into their beds
until nothing but roses nose the blues between lake
10   and garden, lake and sky, the lapse of lawn
where a party could be if those who lived here once
returned to pour the wine. She'd be the sort
to tuck a bud behind her ear, and he to catch
one in his teeth. But alas, we're guests
15   of the present, expectant and sultry; all
graciousness is fled, and rain fills the spent
blooms, tumbles their tops, weighted with ruffles
and shocks of pink. The gardener too disappears
with his breeches the color of mustard and cinched
20   with a string, gone back into the pages of Hardy
or Lawrence. Perhaps, he'll appear again Tuesday next,
but he won't look any of us living in the eye.

By Leslie Adrienne Miller

→ CHALLENGE
1. How would you describe the voice and situation in 'The Dead Send Their Gardener'?
2. What is the poet's attitude towards the man in the poem?
3. The poet and the man seem close in some respects but distant in others – what is it that divides them?
4. Can you identify any similarities and differences between this poem and 'A Peasant' on page 15. Pay particular attention each poet's approach as well as his/her attitudes as expressed through the use of character.

SECTION I EXAMINED UNITS 17

Upgrade panels
These colour-coded panels show you what is expected of a grade B, A or A* answer and help you to understand the differences between these grades.

Source texts
Poems and extracts provide opportunities to practise your skills.

Challenge activity boxes
This book is filled with challenging activities to help you broaden your skills and improve your understanding of English Literature.

Upgrade

Throughout the book and at the end of every chapter, you will find colour-coded **Upgrade panels**. This feature is designed to help you improve your work and move up through the grades. Each panel focuses on a particular part of the assessment and explains what is expected of a grade B, A and A* answer.

A* ↑	The response explores the Shakespeare play and the poetry with a similar level of detail. Links and points of comparison are clearly expressed, well organized and developed. The student is able to cross-reference between texts effectively.
A ↑	The response deals with both the Shakespeare play and poetry in detail. Links are clearly expressed and relevant to the theme. The student is also able to use cross-reference to make points.
B	The response deals with both the Shakespeare play and poetry. Links are relevant to the task and are explained.

Small Upgrade panels

The panel on the left focuses on making links between texts. Small panels like this appear throughout each chapter. These panels may be linked to other features on the page such as activities, sample tasks and sample answers.

Full-page Upgrade panels

At the end of each chapter, you will find a full-page Upgrade panel. This is designed to help you assess your own practice answers and extended writing.

At the end of each chapter you will find an extended task to complete. Once you have completed it, you can use the Upgrade panel to rate your work. You can then work out what you need to do to improve your performance.

Upgrade self-assessment panels
Full page self-assessment panels help you to rate your work and identify where you can improve.

Practice exam questions
Based on the format of actual exam papers, these practice questions allow you to test what you have learned.

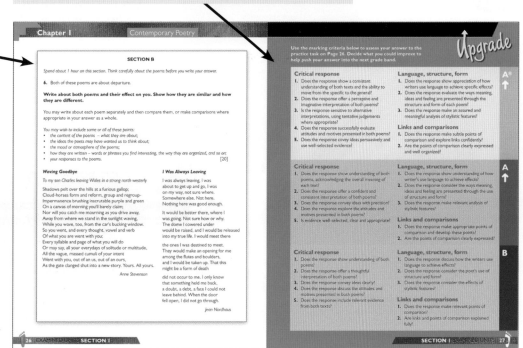

Chapter 1   Contemporary Poetry

Aim for A

- When writing about poetry, you are able to produce a consistently thoughtful and focused analysis.
- You are able to write about the detail of the poems.
- You are able to explore meaning through confident and insightful discussion of language, structure and poetic techniques.
- You are able to make confident points of comparison.

Aim for A*

- Your analysis of the poems is skilful and assured.
- You are able to write about the detail of the poems, prioritizing and organizing your points to ensure balanced coverage of both poems.
- You are able to reveal meaning through perceptive discussion of language, structure and poetic techniques.
- You are able to make sensitive and sustained points of comparison.

Reading poetry

The secret to writing well about poetry is to read as many poems as possible and to talk about them freely. It is important to discuss and compare ideas about poetry whenever you can, so that you can adopt a questioning approach to reading and responding to any poem. This will help you to feel prepared when you come to write about **unseen** poems on your own in the exam.

Studying unseen poetry in the exam means reading and responding in writing to two poems that you probably have not seen before. At some point in your response, you will be expected to compare the two poems.

You need to read both poems and get a hold on both of them before you write. They will both be **contemporary** poems. To reach the top grades, you need to show that you are not intimidated by poetry, and that you can write about poetry just as well as you can write about any other kind of text.

You need to explore and analyse poems confidently, by engaging with ideas and arguments. You need to select and highlight the key details from the texts, but you also need a good grasp of each writer's purpose and motivation for writing.

At the top level, spotting features is not enough. You must engage with the views and arguments in the poems by using your own expression to 'echo' the original writing.

> ## Key words
>
> **Unseen** – An unseen poem is so called because when you face it in the exam, the chances are that you will be seeing it for the first time. In other words, it is not a set poem that you have to revise.

> ## Key words
>
> **Contemporary** – Texts relevant to our current age, although they may have been written during the last millennium; from the latter part of the 20th century right up until the present day.

THE ASSESSMENT

GCSE English Literature Unit 1 Section B

The unseen poetry comparison will be assessed in Section B of your **exam** for Unit 1. Section A of Unit 1 focuses on Different Cultures prose. This part of the exam is covered in Chapter 2.

You will have two hours to complete the entire exam paper for Unit 1, which means you should allow **one hour** to complete the unseen poetry comparison. In preparation for this unit, candidates are advised to study at least fifteen poems, in addition to those studied for Unit 3.

Approaching the exam

Here is one suggested approach to the exam:
- Read and annotate both poems, taking a good 10 to 15 minutes to do so.
- Take note of the lead-in sentence in the exam question; this can help to point you in the right direction.
- Write about the first poem, tracking it for around 20 minutes.
- Turn to the second poem, tracking it for 20 to 25 minutes.
- Make comparisons with the first poem as you track the second poem, noting similarities and differences as they occur to you.
- Allow a few minutes at the end to check your work.

Understanding the task

In the exam you will be presented with the following instructions:

SECTION B

Spend about 1 hour on this section. Think carefully about the poems before you write your answer.

Both of these poems are about…

Write about both poems and their effect on you. Show how they are similar and how they are different.

You may write about each poem separately and then compare them, or make comparisons where appropriate in your answer as a whole.

You may wish to include some or all of these points:
- *the content of the poems – what they are about;*
- *the ideas the poets may have wanted us to think about;*
- *the mood or atmosphere of the poems;*
- *how they are written – words or phrases you find interesting, the way they are organized, and so on;*
- *your responses to the poems.*

Take this guidance seriously and judge your time wisely.

This lead-in sentence will relate directly to the poems — pay attention to what it tells you!

Make sure you cover both poems in your answer.

Try to consider all of these topics. You can use these points to structure your writing.

Tracking the text

While every poem is different, each one has a beginning, middle and an end. You need to be businesslike and, if you like, a little unpoetic, in the way that you approach your reading and study. Read each poem one sentence at a time, tentatively exploring the meaning.

In the exam, you should read the poems with a pen in your hand, indicating words and phrases that strike you and add to your understanding of what the poet is trying to say. You should also be sensitive to **ambiguity** and points that could be open to different interpretations. To achieve the highest grades, you need to be prepared to form your own opinions. You need to think for yourself, trust your instincts and be prepared to justify your views. Practise these skills by reading and engaging with the poems that follow.

'Introduction to Poetry' by Billy Collins is something of a heartfelt plea by a poet about how to respond to poetry and also how not to do it! 'Eating Poetry' by Mark Strand is another example of a poet writing about poetry and indeed celebrating it in a spectacular way.

Key words

Ambiguity – Something that can have more than one meaning – very often a deliberate intention in poetry! Be sensitive to these possibilities as you read. However, be careful not to overcomplicate where something is frank and obvious.

Introduction to Poetry

I ask them to take a poem
and hold it up to the light
like a color slide

or press an ear against its hive.

5 I say drop a mouse into a poem
and watch him probe his way out,

or walk inside the poem's room
and feel the walls for a light switch.

I want them to waterski
10 across the surface of a poem
waving at the author's name on the shore.

But all they want to do
is tie the poem to a chair with rope
and torture a confession out of it.

15 They begin beating it with a hose
to find out what it really means.

By Billy Collins

Eating Poetry

Ink runs from the corners of my mouth.
There is no happiness like mine.
I have been eating poetry.

The librarian does not believe what she sees.
5 Her eyes are sad
and she walks with her hands in her dress.

The poems are gone.
The light is dim.
The dogs are on the basement stairs
and coming up.

10 Their eyeballs roll,
their blond legs burn like brush.
The poor librarian begins to stamp her
feet and weep.

She does not understand.
When I get on my knees and lick her hand,
15 she screams.

I am a new man.
I snarl at her and bark.
I romp with joy in the bookish dark.

By Mark Strand

→ CHALLENGE

1. Read 'Introduction to Poetry'. What are the poet's thoughts and feelings about how students often respond to poems?
2. Read 'Eating Poetry'. How does the poet try to persuade the reader to enjoy poetry?
3. What impressions do you have of the librarian?
4. Can you identify any similarities between the two poems, perhaps in terms of subject matter, tone or approach?

Now read another pair of poems. 'Not Yet My Mother' by Owen Sheers reveals the poet looking at a photo of his mother as a young woman.

Not Yet My Mother

Yesterday I found a photo
of you at seventeen,
holding a horse and smiling,
not yet my mother.

5   The tight riding hat hid your hair,
and your legs were still the long shins of a boy's.
You held the horse by the halter,
your hand a fist under its huge jaw.

The blown trees were still in the background
10 and the sky was grained by the old film stock,
but what caught me was your face,
which was mine.

And I thought, just for a second, that you were me.
But then I saw the woman's jacket,
15 nipped at the waist, the ballooned jodhpurs,
and of course the date, scratched in the corner.

All of which told me again,
that this was you at seventeen, holding a horse
and smiling, not yet my mother,
20 although I was clearly already your child.

By Owen Sheers

→ **CHALLENGE**

1. How would you describe the poet's thoughts and feelings in this poem?
    Write a paragraph giving your overall view and pick out one or two examples
    to illustrate how the poet conveys these feelings to the reader.
2. What ideas does the poet want you to think about? What wider issues does
    the poet raise as he considers his mother's photo?

'Maiden Name' by Philip Larkin explores the ideas and consequences of a woman changing her name when she marries.

Maiden Name

Marrying left your maiden name disused.
Its five light sounds no longer mean your face,
Your voice, and all your variants of grace;
For since you were so thankfully confused
5   By law with someone else, you cannot be
Semantically the same as that young beauty:
It was of her that these two words were used.

Now it's a phrase applicable to no one,
Lying just where you left it, scattered through
10 Old lists, old programmes, a school prize or two
Packets of letters tied with tartan ribbon –
Then is it scentless, weightless, strengthless, wholly
Untruthful? Try whispering it slowly.
No, it means you. Or, since you're past and gone,

15 It means what we feel now about you then:
How beautiful you were, and near, and young,
So vivid, you might still be there among
Those first few days, unfingermarked again.
So your old name shelters our faithfulness,
20 Instead of losing shape and meaning less
With your depreciating luggage laden.

By Philip Larkin

→ **CHALLENGE**

1. How and why does the poet argue for the importance of a woman's maiden name?
2. Are there any parallels between this poem and 'Not Yet My Mother'? Does the poet deal with any similar themes?
3. How does Philip Larkin's perspective differ in this poem from that of Owen Sheers?

Openings – voice and situation

Even though some poems, or poets, will speak to you very directly, be a little cautious when dealing with the 'unseen'. You cannot be sure that you are on top of your game at all times, but you can avoid being horribly wrong by reading carefully, especially when reading the opening of a poem.

Try to work out the **voice** and **situation**. Who is speaking – the poet or a character? And what is happening in the poem? As in prose, poems may have first-person and third-person 'speakers', whether this is the voice of the poet or that of a character known as a 'persona'. The situation may appear straightforward or deliberately problematic; however, you should be sensitive to multiple interpretations as you read.

Look at the opening lines from four poems, below, and answer the questions that follow.

> **Key words**
>
> **Voice** – Poets can speak as themselves or as a character. Another term for voice is 'register', which refers to the features of the language used by the speaker.

Introduction to Poetry

I ask them to take a poem
and hold it up to the light
like a color slide

or press an ear against its hive.

Billy Collins

Not Yet My Mother

Yesterday I found a photo
of you at seventeen,
holding a horse and smiling,
not yet my mother.

Owen Sheers

Eating Poetry

Ink runs from the corners of my mouth.

Mark Strand

Maiden Name

Marrying left your maiden name disused.

Philip Larkin

→ CHALLENGE

1. Who is speaking in 'Introduction to Poetry'? Who do you think 'them' refers to?
2. What is the impact of the first line of 'Eating Poetry'?
3. What is it that captures the poet's interest in 'Not Yet My Mother'?
4. What is problematic about the opening of 'Maiden Name'? Could there be some ambiguity here?
5. Now look at the other poems throughout this chapter and explore their openings.

Key words

Situation – What is going on in the poem? How would you sum up the overall subject matter, direction and message? Top-grade responses will show a grasp of each poem in its entirety as well as showing sensitivity to detail.

Endings

Do not expect the last line of the poem to deliver the meaning. Look for the last coherent sentence and work with it. Whatever you uncover, remember to judge it in the context of the poem as a whole. How do the last lines relate to the rest of the poem? Do they draw together the ideas expressed in the poem? Or does the ending take a different turn?

Read the poems that follow and consider, in each case, what the poet attempts to convey in the final lines. 'The Road Not Taken' by Robert Frost looks at choices that we have to make as we travel through life. 'Book Ends' by Tony Harrison is a poem about the relationship between a son (the poet) and his parents.

The Road Not Taken

Two roads diverged in a yellow wood,
And sorry I could not travel both
And be one traveler, long I stood
And looked down one as far as I could
5 To where it bent in the undergrowth;

Then took the other, as just as fair,
And having perhaps the better claim,
Because it was grassy and wanted wear;
Though as for that the passing there
10 Had worn them really about the same,

And both that morning equally lay
In leaves no step had trodden black.
Oh, I kept the first for another day!
Yet knowing how way leads on to way,
15 I doubted if I should ever come back.

I shall be telling this with a sigh
Somewhere ages and ages hence:
Two roads diverged in a wood, and I –
I took the one less traveled by,
20 And that has made all the difference.

By Robert Frost

Book Ends

Baked the day she suddenly dropped dead
we chew it slowly that last apple pie.

Shocked into sleeplessness you're scared of bed.
We never could talk much, and now don't try.

5 *You're like book ends, the pair of you, she'd say,*
Hog that grate, say nothing, sit, sleep, stare...

The 'scholar' me, you, worn out on poor pay,
only our silence made us seem a pair.

Not as good for staring in, blue gas,
10 too regular each bud, each yellow spike.

A night you need my company to pass
and she not here to tell us we're alike!

Your life's all shattered into smithereens.

Back in our silences and sullen looks,
15 for all the Scotch we drink, what's still between's
not the thirty or so years, but books, books, books.

By Tony Harrison

Avoid

Don't overwrite or contradict yourself. Make a point and move on.

STORM OF GLORY

→ **CHALLENGE**

1. How do the endings of 'The Road Not Taken' and 'Book Ends' resolve each poem?
2. What thoughts and feelings does the poet convey at the end of each poem?
3. Can you identify any links between these poems? Are there any similarities, for example, in how these poems are structured? What is the function of the final stanza in each case?
4. Explore other final statements from all the poems in this chapter. Make comparisons wherever you can make sensible connections.

Characters in poems

Like any other form of literature, poems can include characters and, where you find them, they will be worthy of comment. Poets may present you with a full detailed description of an individual, as in 'A Peasant' by R S Thomas, below. Alternatively, you may discover only fragments of detail or an incomplete picture.

When reading poetry, you will often build your knowledge of the characters based on limited information. You will rely on informed assumptions, feelings, suggestions – all of which form part of your personal response. To achieve the highest grades, any discussion of characters needs to be focused on the poet's approach and intentions. Exploring characters in poetry often leads the reader to broader issues that stretch beyond the literal presentation of the individual in the poem.

A Peasant

Iago Prytherch his name, though, be it allowed,
Just an ordinary man of the bald Welsh hills,
Who pens a few sheep in a gap of cloud.
Docking mangels, chipping the green skin
5 From the yellow bones with a half-witted grin
Of satisfaction, or churning the crude earth
To a stiff sea of clods that glint in the wind –
So are his days spent, his spittled mirth
Rarer than the sun that cracks the cheeks
10 Of the gaunt sky perhaps once in a week.
And then at night see him fixed in his chair
Motionless, except when he leans to gob in the fire.
There is something frightening in the vacancy of his mind.
His clothes, sour with years of sweat
15 And animal contact, shock the refined,
But affected, sense with their stark naturalness.
Yet this is your prototype, who, season by season
Against siege of rain and the wind's attrition,
Preserves his stock, an impregnable fortress
20 Not to be stormed even in death's confusion.
Remember him, then, for he, too, is a winner of wars,
Enduring like a tree under the curious stars.

By R S Thomas

→ CHALLENGE

1. How does the poet present the character of Iago Prytherch and what is his attitude towards him?
2. What is your reaction to the character? What aspects of the poet's description have the biggest impact on you?

The following student answers focus on how R S Thomas presents Iago as well as the poet's **attitude** towards the character. Read both responses and identify what each student does well and how each student might improve.

> Iago Prytherch is part of the land, part of the scenery. It is a portrait in words of a Welsh hill farmer; primitive compared with a city-dweller. He is a hero in his way. There is a sense of time running slowly.

> 'A Peasant' opens with the mention of Iago Prytherch, whose name sounds as harsh as the tough, uncompromising landscape he works with. Thomas writes with a combination of compassion, admiration and distaste within the poem. Thomas uses brutish descriptions of Iago – 'spittled mirth', 'he leans to gob in the fire', 'half-witted grin'. The 'frightening vacancy' of Iago's mind emphasizes to the reader his inability to account for his situation. It is a harsh life as a Welsh hill farmer, and an unchanging one, but Iago is a fighter and a winner. His type will endure as long as the Welsh landscape.

→ CHALLENGE

1. What are the strengths of each response?
2. How could each student perhaps improve their analysis?
3. Use the **Upgrade** panel below to rate each response and then discuss your decision with a partner. Do you agree on the grade you have awarded? Why/Why not?

Upgrade

A* ↑ The student gives a confident and perceptive analysis of how the poet conveys the character of Iago. As well as dealing with precise detail, the student is able to write about Iago's character as a whole, touching on the wider themes and issues to which the character is connected. The student is also sensitive to the poet's feelings about the character, identifying potential complexities in tone and language.

A ↑ The student gives a confident analysis of how the poet conveys the character of Iago, making precise reference to the detail of the text. The student is also aware of the wider significance of the character and how it relates to other ideas in the poem. The student is able to successfully judge and comment on the poet's feelings about the character.

B The student is able to make relevant comments about how the poet presents the character of Iago based on the detail of the text. The student is able to identify the poet's feelings about the character and show how these are conveyed to the reader.

Key words

Attitude – What does the writer feel about the subject matter in the poem? What are his/her opinions and how can you tell? Higher-level responses show a keen awareness of the writer's feelings and how these are conveyed.

Now read 'The Dead Send Their Gardener' by Leslie Adrienne Miller and complete the tasks that follow. Miller's poem describes a man who appears to belong to a different age.

The Dead Send Their Gardener

He arrives in the courtyard with two cartons
of juice, each of which he'll tip and drain
at one go in the heat, and a sack of food
for the roses. He looms over his tools,
5   blond and dusty as a stalk of ripe wheat,
surely someone's prized lover. Centuries
bask among his hybrid teas, and he shakes
his capable handfuls of food into their beds
until nothing but roses nose the blues between lake
10 and garden, lake and sky, the lapse of lawn
where a party could be if those who lived here once
returned to pour the wine. She'd be the sort
to tuck a bud behind her ear, and he to catch
one in his teeth. But alas, we're guests
15 of the present, expectant and sultry; all
graciousness is fled, and rain fills the spent
blooms, tumbles their tops, weighted with ruffles
and shocks of pink. The gardener too disappears
with his breeches the color of mustard and cinched
20 with a string, gone back into the pages of Hardy
or Lawrence. Perhaps, he'll appear again Tuesday next,
but he won't look any of us living in the eye.

By Leslie Adrienne Miller

→ CHALLENGE

1. How would you describe the voice and situation in 'The Dead Send Their Gardener'?
2. What is the poet's attitude towards the man in the poem?
3. The poet and the man seem close in some respects but distant in others – what is it that divides them?
4. Can you identify any similarities and differences between this poem and 'A Peasant' on page 15? Pay particular attention to each poet's approach as well as his/her attitudes as expressed through the use of character.

Writing about the poet's ideas and intentions

You should be sensitive to the fact that poetry can often vary in terms of its **purpose**. Poets write for all kinds of reasons: to expose, to celebrate, to entertain, to protest. Sometimes there are multiple reasons and sometimes these reasons overlap.

You should not rely on the powers of guesswork to determine the writer's intentions. Read both poems in full. As you read, ask yourself what the poet is expecting from you as a reader. Are you encouraged to laugh, to agree, to question? Do you feel involved or remote?

The next two poems are very different in terms of subject matter, but also in terms of purpose. 'All-Purpose Poem for State Occasions', by Wendy Cope, is a poem that declares what it is in the title, but how seriously readers respond is up to them.

Key words

Purpose – The intentions behind the writing. High-level responses will be sensitive to these ideas and motivations.

All-Purpose Poem for State Occasions

The nation rejoices or mourns
As this happy or sombre day dawns.
Our eyes will be wet
As we sit round the set,
5 Neglecting our flowerbeds and lawns.

As Her Majesty rides past the crowd
They'll be silent or cheer very loud
But whatever they do
It's undoubtedly true
10 That they'll feel patriotic and proud.

In Dundee and Penzance and Ealing
We're imbued with appropriate feeling:
We're British and loyal
And love every royal
15 And tonight we shall drink till we're reeling.

By Wendy Cope

→ CHALLENGE

1. What could you safely say about the opening couplet?
2. What are your thoughts and feelings about the ideas in this poem and the way they are expressed?
3. Does the poet give a positive or negative opinion of 'state occasions'?

'Wind' by Ted Hughes explores the experience of sitting out a persistent gale. Quite a different subject matter entirely! But Hughes also sets out to engage the reader in a different way. His powerful use of imagery, and lines filled with activity and movement, work to engulf the reader so they too share a very vivid, personal experience of the storm.

Wind

This house has been far out at sea all night,
The woods crashing through darkness, the booming hills,
Winds stampeding the fields under the window
Floundering black astride and blinding wet

5   Till day rose; then under an orange sky
The hills had new places, and wind wielded
Blade-light, luminous black and emerald,
Flexing like the lens of a mad eye.

At noon I scaled along the house-side as far as
10 The coal-house door. Once I looked up—
Through the brunt wind that dented the balls of my eyes
The tent of the hills drummed and strained its guyrope,

The fields quivering, the skyline a grimace,
At any second to bang and vanish with a flap:
15 The wind flung a magpie away and a black-
Back gull bent like an iron bar slowly. The house

Rang like some fine green goblet in the note
That any second would shatter it. Now deep
In chairs, in front of the great fire, we grip
20 Our hearts and cannot entertain book, thought,

Or each other. We watch the fire blazing,
And feel the roots of the house move, but sit on,
Seeing the window tremble to come in,
Hearing the stones cry out under the horizons.

By Ted Hughes

→ **CHALLENGE**

1. How does the poet make the scene in this poem tense and dramatic?
2. What makes the experience of the storm vivid to the reader?
3. Are the poet's views important in this poem? Or is there a different focus?

In the following piece of A* writing, a student assesses the ideas and intentions presented in 'Wind', considering the language and also the possible wider meanings of the situation that occurs in the poem. Read the answer with a partner and identify what makes this response so effective.

> There is a pervading and unrelenting sense of violence throughout the poem. It is present in the first stanza with 'the woods crashing through darkness' and in the last line with, 'the stones cry out under the horizons'.
>
> Furthermore, this violence is not portrayed as a show of pure strength, but a physical threat. Hughes uses the disturbing image of the wind: 'Flexing like the lens of a mad eye', which gives it a malevolent, almost vindictive persona. The threat is clearly present in the language used by the poet. Particularly effective, I thought, is the end of the second line of the fourth stanza, 'vanish with a flap'. The extremely short vowel in 'flap' highlights the swift, sudden violence of the wind and the pause prompted by the colon following it emphasizes this, like an explicit menace.
>
> The description of 'a black-/Back gull bent like an iron bar slowly' also hints at this wind's malign nature. The unexpected position of 'slowly' makes the line slow and difficult to read, perhaps mirroring the bird's tortuous struggle against the wind.
>
> In 'Wind', man is belittled and humbled; brought down to the level of the rest of nature by the power of the wind, hence the metaphor of the house as a tree: 'the roofs of the house move'. All man's efforts to impose himself on the world, represented by the house, are fragile and vulnerable like 'some fine green goblet' that could shatter 'any second'. This implies the wind could be symbolic of fate, capable of ruining the best made plan, or a warning against human complacency, that we cannot dominate or control completely either nature or chance.
>
> Furthermore, the violence of the wind is parallel to the tension inside the house, where the inhabitants 'grip' their hearts. However, the sheer differences in scale hint at the irrelevance of these people in the face of such great power.

→ CHALLENGE

1. What, in your opinion, makes this response stand out as a high-quality piece of writing? Use the **Upgrade** panel below to help you.
2. Do you agree with this student's interpretation of 'Wind'? Could you offer an alternative perspective to any of the views offered?

Upgrade

A* ↑	The response deals skilfully with the detail of the language and explores the wider meaning of the poem. Evidence is expertly chosen and the overall piece of writing is persuasive and convincing.
A ↑	The response pays close attention to the poet's use of language and the overall meaning of the poem. Evidence is well selected and relevant and the writing is clear and well structured.
B	The response deals with the detail of language and shows good overall understanding of the poem. Evidence is relevant and the writing is clear and accurate.

Key words

Prioritize – This means writing about the most important points first. It requires you to think ahead in terms of the points you wish to make and to be disciplined in your writing. Once you have made a point – move on. You will not be rewarded for it twice!

Details of language

It is difficult and maybe unwise to give wholesale advice about dealing with the details of language in an 'unseen' poem. You have to develop confidence through experience, and learn how and when to be cautious or assertive in explaining a word or phrase within a whole sentence.

In the exam you will have the freedom to write about any aspect of language within the poems you are responding to. However, you should use this freedom wisely. Top-grade answers will be selective and will **prioritize** the most interesting points. Use your judgement to select the aspects of the poems most worthy of comment.

Use the wording of the task to guide you, but be prepared to lead the way in terms of what appeals to you, or moves you, or surprises you. This is the opposite to feature-spotting and is key to forming a true personal response to poetry.

Look back at the poems you have covered so far in this chapter and answer the questions below.

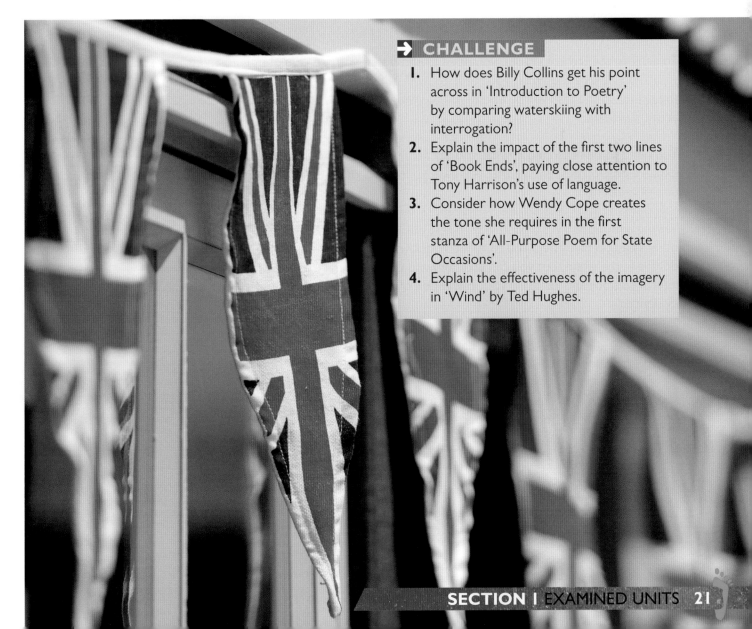

→ CHALLENGE

1. How does Billy Collins get his point across in 'Introduction to Poetry' by comparing waterskiing with interrogation?
2. Explain the impact of the first two lines of 'Book Ends', paying close attention to Tony Harrison's use of language.
3. Consider how Wendy Cope creates the tone she requires in the first stanza of 'All-Purpose Poem for State Occasions'.
4. Explain the effectiveness of the imagery in 'Wind' by Ted Hughes.

Giving a personal response

What is a personal response? Here is what some other students had to say:

> *Every opinion I have about a poem is a personal response to it.*

> *It's my reaction. How the poem makes me feel.*

> *Whether I like or dislike the poem.*

> *It means no copying.*

> *It's my interpretation – it's what I think the poem means and why.*

→ CHALLENGE

1. Discuss the comments above with a partner. Which ones do you agree or disagree with?
2. Which comments describe a basic level of personal response and which represent higher-level skills?

To achieve the highest grades, you need to show that you are confident in forming your own views about what you read. You will not have studied the poems before the exam, so the task will be asking you to give your immediate thoughts and feelings about the texts.

You need to be reasoned in what you say and, whilst you should think freely and explore possibilities, ensure that you base your views on a sensible reading of each unit of meaning.

Talking about poetry is a good way to test out your ideas, and hearing the views of others can certainly help you to refine your own thoughts. You will not be able to do this in the exam, but you can take forward the experience of exploring multiple interpretations and justifying your own point of view through selection and use of evidence.

> **Avoid**
>
> Don't base your answer on feature-spotting. Write about the things that matter!

→ CHALLENGE

1. Choose one of the tasks below and make a list of key points in response to the question.
   a) Read 'The Road Not Taken' on page 13. How does the poet try to make you think about making decisions about the future?
   b) Read 'Book Ends' on page 14. What makes this scene so emotive in the poem?
2. Get into a pair or group with other students that have chosen to do the same task. Discuss your ideas.
3. Having discussed the poems, decide which of your points are the most convincing and number them in order of priority.

Comparisons

It is rare that a poem is written by a poet expressly for the purpose of comparing it to another poem. However, comparison is an important requirement of the unseen poetry exam.

Key words

Cross-reference – A cross-reference is a link. It might be a link between the poems or a link between points you have made about them.

Top-grade comparisons are characterized by good organization and perceptive thinking. Think ahead about the points you wish to make and structure your thoughts coherently. Only make a comparison where you have a valid point to make and develop your points fully. Use **cross-reference** to identify links between the texts. However, don't waste time playing Ping-Pong between the poems!

Read the following grade A answer comparing 'Introduction to Poetry' by Billy Collins with 'Eating Poetry' by Mark Strand. Both of these poems are about writing and reading poetry. The comments from the examiner highlight what this student does well.

The first paragraph shows evidence of reflection, carefully moving forward sentence by sentence, making valid points and earning credit.

The student is confident about the poet's message here: students have to get stuck into poetry; reading blankly is not enough.

This paragraph (appreciating the irony) is very astute, and cleverly notices the whole dilemma of the poem, and the exam exercise. The student also notes how squeezing every last drop of speculative meaning from a poem is not good either as this kills the pleasure of reading and exploring.

> ### 'Introduction to Poetry' and 'Eating Poetry'
>
> 'Introduction to Poetry' by Billy Collins is about how he thinks people should read poetry. It is a simple, light-hearted poem about reading a poem and trying to understand its meaning. You hold a color slide up to the light to see the picture clearly, and when you hold a poem up to the light, with interest and an open mind, it is to see the meaning of the poem. He also asks for people to listen to someone reading it, or listen to the narrator of the poem, the character and what they're trying to get across: 'press an ear against its hive'. He tells people to get into the poem and hear everything that is going on.
>
> He talks about how easy it is to get lost in a poem. 'I say drop a mouse into a poem/and watch him probe his way out'.
>
> He doesn't mind if they fumble with the meaning, as if they are feeling in a dark room for a light switch.
>
> The teacher is saying that he wants his students 'to waterski/across the surface' as if he wants them to briefly look over it and go with their first ideas.
>
> However students are not wanting to do that. Reading this poem under the conditions I'm writing in makes the poem seem very ironic because I'm doing exactly what the poem is suggesting. In a way it makes me feel guilty 'and torture a confession out of it'. I feel it is very clever, the first five stanzas are all saying the same things but they are said differently.
>
> But at the end it says 'They begin beating it with a hose/to find out what it really means'. That suggests that people try to find the meaning without enjoying the poem which isn't how Billy Collins wants them to read his poems. 'Beating' makes analysing a poem seem like a violent action. He wants readers to enjoy the poem like waterskiing and 'waving'. But in reality, students want to tie the poem up.

The second poem 'Eating Poetry' is a slightly crazy poem about reading poetry and how it has an effect on you. The title shows that this person loves poems a lot, and it is as if they would 'eat' them greedily like they cannot get enough. This is also backed up by the line 'there is no happiness like mine'. 'Ink runs from the corners of my mouth' suggests to me that the reader has devoured lots of poems and is a noisy and messy eater. The way the librarian came across made me think she was more traditional and possibly wants her library quiet and orderly.

The poet shows wild imagination and the situation cannot be explained literally. Mark Strand has written the poem as if he is transformed into a dog. He is trying to get across the idea that poetry can change you, and make strange things happen. It can make you think outside the box, while the librarian is trying to look after her library according to the rules.

There are strange images of dogs and the librarian definitely is upset. It is as if she is having a nightmare. But the narrator as a dog is friendly and wants to 'lick her hand'.

The narrator is content at the end as if he has had a filling meal: 'I am a new man'. But he probably scares the librarian because he snarls and barks. After eating poetry, he is definitely happy and wild, romping with joy.

The two poems are both about reading and writing poetry and how people perceive it. These two poems are very similar in the fact that they are both stating messages about poetry itself. 'Introduction to Poetry' is showing the simplicity of finding a meaning in a poem and how you just need to read it before thinking of ideas. 'Eating Poetry' is showing the different effects writing poetry has on you, a bit like music does.

However they are displaying different messages altogether. The poem written by Billy Collins tells the reader in depth about the enjoyment of poetry. The title 'Introduction to Poetry' also suggests that it is a poem trying to tell people who haven't read or enjoyed poetry how to read it. 'Introduction to Poetry' helps us more as students, because I can understand the images one by one. 'Eating Poetry' worries students I think because it is chaotic and confusing, even though it creates a humorous scene.

The student hits the right button by describing 'Eating Poetry' as 'slightly crazy'. The pivotal word, though, is 'devoured', which successfully covers all meanings of 'eating', both literal and metaphorical. Perfect.

The student offers a thoughtful but entirely rational interpretation of this part of the poem.

The writer fuses the language of the poem into the language of the response, tracking briskly but methodically.

Arguably nothing new to be said in the comparison, but the writer shows the skill of juxtaposing the main ideas.

The writer is still going forward and, with a mix of personal response and ironic awareness again, ends with a profound truth about the difference between the two poems.

'Introduction to Poetry' and 'Eating Poetry' are easily accessible poems in terms of language – they are not dense or complex – but they are difficult poems to explain. This student has done an excellent job of delving into the meaning of the poems and expresses interpretations that are both thoughtful and realistic and also grounded in the words of the text.

This response stands out because the student has confidently grasped the writer's intentions as expressed in each poem. It also succeeds in conveying a degree of personal feeling that supports and indeed enhances the ongoing analysis. This is a grade A* response.

Wider reading

It goes without saying that the best way to prepare for this part of the course is to read a lot of poetry. This may mean that you have to do some extra reading in your own time, to build on what you have covered in lessons.

The best way to read poetry is to do it in short bites. Pick one poem and spend some time with it. You do not have to make extensive notes, but you should read with a questioning attitude and invest some thought in the experience. One way to do this is to discuss the poems with another student in your class.

> **→ CHALLENGE**
>
> Find two contemporary poems that you have read and enjoyed and would recommend to others. Be prepared to explain what interests you about them and why they appealed to you.

Final word

What makes a high-level response to unseen poetry?

When responding to two previously unseen poems in an exam, top-grade students will read and explore the poems patiently, and respond with a mixture of caution and confidence. They will establish a secure sense of the voice and the immediate context of each poem and go forward carefully without wild speculation.

Top-grade students will demonstrate good judgement in terms of their own use of language. They will recognize the potential for alternative interpretations in poetry and use tentative language to convey their own views. Their response to each poem will present a good balance of detail and overview and they will be able to make sensible unobtrusive comparisons between the two poems.

Further task

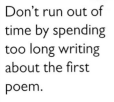

Avoid ⚠

Don't run out of time by spending too long writing about the first poem.

Your exam for Unit 1 will be divided into two sections. Section A will focus on Different Cultures prose. This part of the exam is covered in Chapter 2.

Section B of the exam will ask you to compare **two** previously unseen poems. You should spend **one hour** on this part of the exam.

Complete the task on the next page as if attempting it in the real exam. Spend a full hour on your answer. Once you have completed your response, use the **Upgrade** criteria on page 27 to grade your work.

Use the criteria to work out what you need to do to improve. Write down three changes that could help you to boost your answer into the next grade band or allow you to secure a stronger A*.

SECTION B

Spend about 1 hour on this section. Think carefully about the poems before you write your answer.

Both of these poems are about departures.

Write about both poems and their effect on you. Show how they are similar and how they are different.

You may write about each poem separately and then compare them, or make comparisons where appropriate in your answer as a whole.

You may wish to include some or all of these points:
- *the content of the poems – what they are about;*
- *the ideas the poets may have wanted us to think about;*
- *the mood or atmosphere of the poems;*
- *how they are written – words or phrases you find interesting, the way they are organized, and so on;*
- *your responses to the poems.*

[20]

Waving Goodbye

To my son Charles leaving Wales in a strong north westerly

Shadows pelt over the hills at a furious gallop;
Cloud-horses form and reform, group and regroup—
Impermanence brushing inscrutable purple and green
On a canvas of morning you'll barely claim;
Nor will you catch me mourning as you drive away,
Away from where we stand in the sunlight waving,
While you wave, too, from the car's bucking window.

So you went, and every thought, vowel and verb
Of what you are went with you;
Every syllable and page of what you will do
Or may say, all your everydays of solitude or multitude,
All the vague, massed cumuli of your intent
Went with you, out of an us, out of an ours,
As the gate clanged shut into a new story. Yours. All yours.

Anne Stevenson

I Was Always Leaving

I was always leaving, I was
about to get up and go, I was
on my way, not sure where.
Somewhere else. Not here.
Nothing here was good enough.

It would be better there, where I
was going. Not sure how or why.
The dome I cowered under
would be raised, and I would be released
into my true life. I would meet there

the ones I was destined to meet.
They would make an opening for me
among the flutes and boulders,
and I would be taken up. That this
might be a form of death

did not occur to me. I only know
that something held me back,
a doubt, a debt, a face I could not
leave behind. When the door
fell open, I did not go through.

Jean Nordhaus

Use the marking criteria below to assess your answer to the practice task on page 26. Decide what you could improve to help push your answer into the next grade band.

Critical response

1. Does the response show a consistent understanding of both texts and the ability to move from the specific to the general?
2. Does the response offer a perceptive and imaginative interpretation of both poems?
3. Is the response sensitive to alternative interpretations, using tentative judgements where appropriate?
4. Does the response successfully evaluate attitudes and motives presented in both poems?
5. Does the response convey ideas persuasively and use well-selected evidence?

Language, structure, form

1. Does the response show appreciation of how writers use language to achieve specific effects?
2. Does the response evaluate the ways meaning, ideas and feeling are presented through the structure and form of each poem?
3. Does the response make an assured and meaningful analysis of stylistic features?

Links and comparisons

1. Does the response make subtle points of comparison and explore links confidently?
2. Are the points of comparison clearly expressed and well organized?

A*

Critical response

1. Does the response show understanding of both poems, acknowledging the overall meaning of each text?
2. Does the response offer a confident and consistent interpretation of both poems?
3. Does the response convey ideas with precision?
4. Does the response explore the attitudes and motives presented in both poems?
5. Is evidence well selected, clear and appropriate?

Language, structure, form

1. Does the response show understanding of how writers use language to achieve effects?
2. Does the response consider the ways meaning, ideas and feeling are presented through the use of structure and form?
3. Does the response make relevant analysis of stylistic features?

Links and comparisons

1. Does the response make appropriate points of comparison and develop these points?
2. Are the points of comparison clearly expressed?

A

Critical response

1. Does the response show understanding of both poems?
2. Does the response offer a thoughtful interpretation of both poems?
3. Does the response convey ideas clearly?
4. Does the response discuss the attitudes and motives presented in both poems?
5. Does the response include relevant evidence from both texts?

Language, structure, form

1. Does the response discuss how the writers use language to achieve effects?
2. Does the response consider the poets' use of structure and form?
3. Does the response consider the effects of stylistic features?

Links and comparisons

1. Does the response make relevant points of comparison?
2. Are links and points of comparison explained fully?

B

Chapter 2

Aim for A

- You can write a purposeful response to the question set.
- You have a clear grasp of the characters and plot.
- You have a confident understanding of the whole text as well as the ability to select and comment on appropriate details.
- You have a secure appreciation of the background to texts and a clear sense of the genre.

Aim for A*

- You can produce a tightly argued essay with some individuality and style.
- You can demonstrate an impressive understanding of character and plot.
- You can select evidence from across the text to best support your argument and your ideas about the text as a whole.
- Your contextual understanding is well judged and integrated into your essay.

Reading a novel independently

You will be a much stronger candidate if you are willing to read and study your books at home. If you get to read them independently before your teacher introduces them in class, be confident that your reactions to the story will be relevant and useful for later. You may wish to keep a log of some of your ideas. Top-grade students will be confident when forming views about texts and to succeed in this you need to be an active reader. Reading a text independently is the opposite of being spoon-fed!

You must study **two prose texts** (novels) for your examinations for GCSE English Literature. One text will be a prose text from a different culture and one text will be **either** a contemporary prose text **or** a literary heritage prose text. You will **not** be able to take copies of the novels into your examinations with you.

THE ASSESSMENT

GCSE English Literature Unit 1 Section A

You will be assessed on your study of a Different Cultures prose text in Section A of your **exam** for Unit 1. Section B of this exam focuses on contemporary poetry, which is covered in Chapter 1 of this book.

You will have two hours to complete the entire exam paper for Unit 1, which means you should allow **one hour** to complete the section on Different Cultures prose. In preparation for this unit you should read the entire novel, whether in class or at home.

In the exam you have to answer **two** questions on the novel. The first question (**part (i)**) will require close reading of an <u>extract</u>. Spend 20 minutes on this question. The second question will offer a choice of tasks (**part (ii)** or **part (iii)**) and both will relate to the <u>text as a whole</u>. Spend 40 minutes on your second question.

THE ASSESSMENT

GCSE English Literature Unit 2 Section 2

In Section 2 of your **exam** for Unit 2, you will be assessed on <u>either</u> a contemporary prose text <u>or</u> a literary heritage prose text. Section 1 of this exam focuses on the study of a drama text, which is covered in Chapter 3 of this book.

You will have two hours to complete the entire exam paper for Unit 2, which means you should allow **one hour** to complete the section dealing with the prose text that you have studied.

In the exam you have to answer **two** questions on the novel. The first question (**part (i)**) will require close reading of an <u>extract</u>. Spend 20 minutes on this question. The second question will offer a choice of tasks (**part (ii)** or **part (iii)**) and both will relate to the <u>text as a whole</u>. Spend 40 minutes on your second question.

Your ability to spell, punctuate and use grammar accurately will be assessed in your answer to either question (ii) or question (iii).

Writing about plot

The plot is the sequence of main events in a story. Most novelists aim to create mystery and intrigue in their writing, so the reader should not expect a plot to be simple and straightforward. In many novels, there are several overlapping, interwoven plots – often a main plot with sub-plots.

Novelists use techniques to keep their readers involved and interested. They build anticipation, introduce twists or withhold particular details until the end of the story. Sometimes certain plot points may remain unclear even at the end of a novel. In these situations, the reader is given the freedom to use their imagination to fill in the gaps.

Avoid	

Don't retell the story. Use your writing to explore and develop meaningful points.

Openings

The opening of a novel will set up certain expectations about what the story is likely to be about. It is also likely to give the reader insight into some of the themes and issues the story is going to deal with.

→ CHALLENGE

1. Explore the following openings to two novels. What do you learn as a potential reader about what each story is likely to be about? What issues do you think each novel is likely to deal with?

2. Look at the opening three pages of the prose text you are studying. Make a list of the key issues raised at the start of the novel. For each issue, note down what is revealed at this point in the story.

Anita and Me

I do not have many memories of my very early childhood, apart from the obvious ones, of course. You know, my windswept, bewildered parents in their dusty Indian village garb standing in the open doorway of a 747, blinking back tears of gratitude and heartbreak as the fog cleared to reveal the sign they had been waiting for, dreaming of, the sign planted in tarmac and emblazoned in triumphant hues of red, blue and white, the sign that said simply, WELCOME TO BRITAIN.

Meera Syal

A Christmas Carol

Marley was dead: to begin with. There is no doubt whatever about that. The register of his burial was signed by the clergyman, the clerk, the undertaker, and the chief mourner. Scrooge signed it: and Scrooge's name was good upon 'Change, for anything he chose to put his hand to. Old Marley was as dead as a door-nail.

Charles Dickens

Endings

Endings will resolve the plot one way or another, although endings may be unexpected or in some ways incomplete. An ending may be incomplete in the sense that it leaves particular questions unanswered, or it may be an entirely open ending. The novelist, however, will use the ending to give his or her 'final word', so do not underestimate the messages that lurk in the final part of the story.

The following paragraph occurs very close to the end of *Resistance* by Owen Sheers. The novel re-imagines the outcome of the Second World War. German forces have invaded Britain. The men in Sarah's community have left home to join the British resistance and a group of German soldiers occupies the village.

Resistance

Sarah stood on the top of the Hatterall ridge and looked back towards the valley, but she could no longer see it. There was nothing but the night below her and the stars and clouds above. Adjusting the strap of her bag and tightening her coat about her waist she walked on, north-west along the ridge, along the border of two countries, the wind flinging itself around her. She hadn't brought any food or water and the summer nights at this height were still cold. She knew she didn't have much time, a couple of days perhaps, but she also knew this was no longer important. It was the looking that mattered. The belief and the looking. These were all that were left now and that was why she walked on along the ridge, blind into the night, clutching her bag tightly to her chest with the accounts book of her letters inside, the last of its pages still unwritten.

Owen Sheers

Heritage novels tend to have endings that tie up the loose ends of the plot. All characters are accounted for. Nineteenth-century novels, in particular, also tend to have a moral resolution. This is where the writer appears to act almost like a teacher, using the story to illustrate how and how not to behave. Sometimes this helps to produce a happy ending.

> **→ CHALLENGE**
> How does Owen Sheers give both a sense of finality and mystery in this paragraph?

→ CHALLENGE

1. What features of the following ending from *Silas Marner* make it seem like a 'happy ending'?
2. Can you identify any 'moral messages' in this ending?

Silas Marner

As the bridal group approached, a hearty cheer was raised in the Rainbow yard; and Ben Winthrop, whose jokes had retained their acceptable flavour, found it agreeable to turn in there and receive congratulations; not requiring the proposed interval of quiet at the Stone-pits before joining the company.

Eppie had a larger garden than she had ever expected there now; and in other ways there had been alterations at the expense of Mr Cass, the landlord, to suit Silas's larger family. For he and Eppie had declared that they would rather stay at the Stone-pits than go to any new home. The garden was fenced with stones on two sides, but in front there was an open fence, through which the flowers shone with answering gladness, as the four united people came within sight of them.

'O father,' said Eppie, 'what a pretty home ours is! I think nobody could be happier than we are.'

George Eliot

→ CHALLENGE

Now explore the ending of the novel you are studying. What is the writer saying at the end of the novel? What message or wider meaning can you take from the fate of the characters?

The following practice exam questions ask you to think about the significance of the opening or ending of the text you have studied. To write a successful answer to this type of question, you need to have a strong grasp of the whole plot and you also need to think critically about how themes and ideas develop in the novel.

> To what extent does the opening of the novel prepare the reader for later events?

> Imagine you are one of the main characters. At the end of the story you look back at the events. Write what you would say.

With a partner, discuss and plan answers to the practice exam questions on page 32 in relation to the text you are studying.

Writing about characters

Characters are created and revealed, sketched and moulded, according to the designs of the writer. Some are absolutely central to the development of a story, while others have a relatively small, but significant role.

To achieve the highest grades, you need to go beyond describing the actions and emotions of characters. You need to focus on how characters function and the techniques that writers use to present characters to the reader.

Nick Hornby uses a third-person narrator in *About a Boy*, but reveals character by getting inside the head of Marcus, 'the oldest 12-year-old in the world'.

Using your own words as far as possible, what do you find out about Marcus from the following extract?

About a Boy

During the night after his first day Marcus woke up every half-hour or so. He could tell from the luminous hands of his dinosaur clock: 10.41, 11.19, 11.55, 12.35, 12.55, 1.31... He couldn't believe he was going to have to go back there the next morning, and the morning after that, and the morning after that and…well, then it would be the weekend, but more or less every morning for the rest of his life, just about. Every time he woke up his first thought was that there must be some kind of way past, or round, or even through, this horrible feeling; whenever he had been upset about anything before, there had usually turned out to be some kind of answer – one that mostly involved telling his mum what was bothering him. But there wasn't anything she could do this time. She wasn't going to move him to another school, and even if she did it wouldn't make a whole lot of difference. He'd still be who he was, and that, it seemed to him, was the basic problem.

Nick Hornby

Judging relationships

Characters rarely exist in isolation. In 'reading' a relationship in literature, you might consider factors such as tension, imbalance or confrontation. In your writing, you should also be able to make judgements about the relative weight and active influence of the individuals, and the impact that one character has on another.

For example, in *Anita and Me*, the main character, Meena, lives next door to Mr and Mrs Christmas. However, knowing Mr and Mrs Christmas are neighbours is only useful if you are able to fit this into your understanding of Meena's childhood and experience of life in Tollington in the 1960s.

Read the extract from a top-grade student answer below. In this answer, the student is able to make a confident judgement about the significance of Mr and Mrs Christmas, especially in terms of Meena's development in the novel.

It is Mr Christmas, looking after his sick wife, who confronts Meena after she has accepted Anita's dare to create mischief outside his house. He comments on the fact she has made a bad choice of friends. Mr and Mrs Christmas are part of a close-knit community that the Patels have moved into, and they show some kindness to the new family, and deserve better than Meena's bad behaviour at this point in the story. The reader gets a glimpse of Meena's guilty conscience, but she is going rapidly downhill, and has a long way to go before she is able to break free of Anita's influence.

→ CHALLENGE

Make a list of the points the student makes, in the response above, that go beyond simply describing characters and plot.

If you can discuss ideas like these with some confidence while keeping close to the details of the text, you will be well on your way to meeting the requirements necessary to achieve the higher grades.

→ CHALLENGE

Choose a minor character from the novel you are studying and link them to the main action and meaning of the novel.
- If you are studying *To Kill a Mockingbird*, there are several to choose from – for example: Dill, Mrs Dubrose or Mr Heck Tate.
- If you are studying *Of Mice and Men*, perhaps Carlson would be a challenge.

Personal response

Top-grade answers are often characterized by a genuinely engaged personal response. Many students underestimate the value of their own feelings and ideas and think that a personal response can be tacked on to the end of an essay as a quick extra. In truth, a focused personal response can hugely enrich a strong piece of writing.

As you build your argument, it is perfectly okay to write 'I think' and 'I feel', although thoughts and feelings can be expressed in different ways too. Without personal response, literature becomes – as you would imagine – impersonal. To achieve the highest grades, you need to show that you can form your own opinions and that you can engage with your text directly.

→ CHALLENGE

Choose one of the practice exam questions below. With a partner, plan a response to it in relation to the text you are studying.

> Which character do you have most sympathy for and why?

> Which character do you think changes the most in the novel and why?

Writing about themes

Key words

Themes – Themes are ideas, topics and areas of discussion that run through the text.

In the exam, you may be asked to write about a specific **theme** in the novel. You can identify possible themes as you read and engage with your text and make connections across it. Are there any reccuring issues that the author returns to? What messages does the author try to present to the reader throughout the novel?

There are no hard and fast rules about what kind of themes appear in particular types of prose. However, heritage novels from the past often deal with issues connected with social history, but also echo issues that people face in our own times. Contemporary novels deal with issues of the present day in different ways. Novels from different cultures often handle social issues, while also encouraging the reader to look outside the relative comfort of their familiar situation.

In the exam, you may be asked a question about any one of the main themes in the novel you are studying, including how this theme develops. You may be asked to consider how one of the characters is linked to a particular theme or how the writer conveys his or her feelings about the issue to the reader.

→ CHALLENGE

1. Make a list of themes that feature in the novel you are studying. Which themes are most important overall, in your opinion?
2. Choose one of the practice exam tasks below and write three paragraphs in response to it.
3. Swap your work with a partner and use the **Upgrade** panel to rate your partner's work.

In the real exam, a theme will be specified in the question. However, for this task, choose one of the themes you have identified. How is this theme presented in the novel?

How effective is the title of the novel?

Why do you think the novel is still popular today, at the beginning of the 21st century?

Upgrade

A*↑	The answer shows a strong grasp of the text as a whole but also focuses on precise details that help to support points. The answer judges the significance of one or more themes within the novel as well as demonstrating how the writer presents these issues to the reader. The answer considers the writer's attitude as well as how themes link to wider messages in the text.
A↑	The answer shows a good grasp of the text as a whole and also relates to relevant detail in the text. The answer considers the significance of one or more themes and how the writer presents these to the reader.
B	The answer makes reference to relevant events or characters in the text to help support points about themes. The answer makes valid points about how the writer presents these themes to the reader.

Writing about style and structure

Being so involved in a story, or sympathizing with a character, so much that you forget it is fiction, is often the outcome of good literature! However, studying literature invites an extra dimension of response from a reader – an appreciation of the writer and the skills and techniques that he or she has used.

Identifying the writer's style

Put simply, **style** is the words on the page, and **structure** is the way the book is organized. The writer starts with a blank piece of paper and has to decide on a beginning, a middle and an end, which words are best for the occasion and, if you like, which order to put them in!

In any form of literature, style is always very closely linked to the content, as well as the history and culture of the text. The quickest way to raise your awareness of style is to witness an obvious contrast between two very different styles of writing.

Read the extract, below, from *A Christmas Carol* by Charles Dickens, as he describes Christmas Eve in nineteenth-century London.

Key words

Style – Style is the way good writers choose to write, with close attention to word forms and sentences. It is the precision that a quality writer has that is a mark of style.

Key words

Structure – Structure is the way a writer sequences a novel, most obviously in terms of chapters and the way a plot unfolds and characters come and go.

A Christmas Carol

Meanwhile the fog and darkness thickened… The ancient tower of a church, whose gruff old bell was always peeping slyly down at Scrooge out of a gothic window in the wall, became invisible, and struck the hours and quarters in the clouds, with tremulous vibrations afterwards, as if its teeth were chattering in its frozen head up there. The cold became intense. In the main street, at the corner of the court, some labourers were repairing the gas-pipes, and had lighted a great fire in a brazier, round which a party of ragged men and boys were gathered: warming their hands and winking their eyes before the blaze in rapture.

Charles Dickens

In the second extract, from *Paddy Clarke Ha Ha Ha*, the author Roddy Doyle uses a ten-year-old narrator to describe a traumatic situation from a child's perspective. Consider how this extract differs in terms of style.

Paddy Clarke Ha Ha Ha

I never got the chance to run away. I was too late. He left first. The way he shut the door; he didn't slam it. Something; I just knew: he wasn't coming back. He just closed it, like he was going down to the shops, except it was the front door and we only used the front door when people came. He didn't slam it. He closed it behind him – I saw him in the glass. He waited for a few seconds, then went. He didn't have a suitcase or even a jacket, but I knew.

My mouth opened and a roar started but it never came. And a pain in my chest, and I could hear my heart pumping the blood to the rest of me. I was supposed to cry; I thought I was. I sobbed once and that was all.

He'd hit her again and I saw him, and he saw me. He thumped her on the shoulder.

Roddy Doyle

→ **CHALLENGE**

Referring to both extracts, find as many differences as you can in the way the writers use words and sentences. From the knowledge and evidence you have, explain the reasons behind the differences.

Key words

Setting – Setting is the place in which the action of the novel takes place, and usually, of course, there are several specific settings.

Key words

Mood and atmosphere – Characters have moods, and settings have atmosphere. Both refer to emotions expressed in the writing and how these are conveyed to the reader.

Commenting on structure

The structure of a novel can stand out as particularly important in some cases. Several texts end where they begin, which is likely to have a specific impact. In *Of Mice and Men,* Lennie dies at the spot where he and George discussed their future hopes and dreams at the start of the novel. Meanwhile, *Anita and Me* follows a recognizable autobiographical form, ending with Meena going to grammar school and a fairly blunt closure of her relationship with Anita. *Pride and Prejudice* ends with weddings, the end of one story perhaps, and the start of another!

Inevitably, the shape of a novel will be part of its meaning and effect, so regard it as part of your continuing investigation as you study your text. This includes factors such as how events are paced, use of **setting** and how themes and issues are raised and revisited throughout the novel. Right through the grade descriptions, there are references to structure. Candidates are encouraged to recognize how choices in terms of style and structure can influence **mood and atmosphere** and affect how readers react to characters and events.

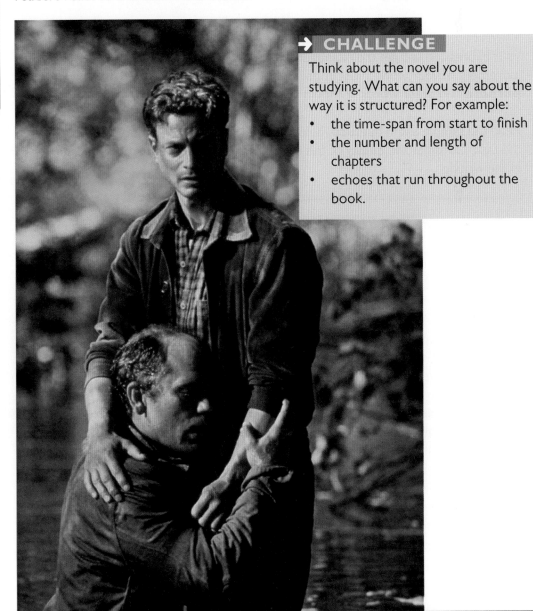

→ **CHALLENGE**

Think about the novel you are studying. What can you say about the way it is structured? For example:

- the time-span from start to finish
- the number and length of chapters
- echoes that run throughout the book.

Understanding the background to texts

The background to a text, or its **context**, includes social, historical and cultural factors. Knowledge of important contexts can enrich a good-quality answer, but only if comments are connected to an understanding of the text. For example, in *To Kill a Mockingbird*, it would be highly appropriate to show an understanding of Maycomb in the early 20th century to explain the treatment of black people in America at this time. However, this understanding should be integrated into the essay, not attached to the beginning or end.

→ CHALLENGE

Refer to the text you are studying. Explain in a paragraph how the situation and treatment of a character reflect the values of the place and time in the novel. For example, if you are studying *Of Mice and Men*, consider the role of Crooks.

Writing skills

While good reading skills are paramount, the quality of your writing will also play a significant part in your performance in GCSE English Literature. Good control of your expression will get the examiner on your side and will influence the overall judgement of your work. Most important of all, your writing should have a sense of **purpose** – in other words, it should answer the questions as set.

Read the sample exam question, below, and an extract from a student response to the task. Consider the quality of this student's expression and the sense of purpose in the writing.

> To what extent do you find '*To Kill a Mockingbird*' an effective title for the novel?

The title of the novel is effective because it shows how human beings can be cruel towards others who are innocent. Tom Robinson is the obvious victim in the novel. However, the other significant 'mockingbird' is Boo Radley, who is supposedly a monster of a man: 'his eyes popped and he drooled'. Like Tom, he thus also becomes a victim of prejudice, as the children build up elaborate lies about him: 'He died years ago and they stuffed him up a chimney'.

Even an adult, albeit the gossipy and prejudiced Miss Stephanie, claims she saw him staring at her through her window one night. All this is used against Boo, even though (as with Tom), it is fictitious.

Also, as with Tom, it seems very few people know about the way Boo actually is – and these people are usually those with 'background' or intelligence (Miss Maudie and Atticus). However, at the conclusion of the novel, we see that society has been cruel to the mockingbirds, and has killed one innocent one: Tom's death is compared to the 'senseless slaughter of songbirds'.

1. How well does the writing respond to the question?
2. How could this answer be improved in terms of the quality of expression and the coherence of the writing?

Quality of written communication

All units in English Literature involve extended writing, and you will be assessed on the quality of your written communication within the overall assessment of each unit. In your exam for Unit 2 (a and b), eight additional marks are also available for accurate spelling, punctuation and grammar. Quality of written communication is assessed according to the areas summarized below.

1. Use the **Upgrade** panels below to rate your skills in each area.
2. For each area, identify two things that you could do to improve your performance in order to achieve a better grade.

Clarity of meaning

This relates to the legibility of your writing and the accuracy of your spelling, punctuation and grammar.

Upgrade

WRITING WITH CLARITY	B	→ A	→ A*
How good is your English under pressure?	It might get a little shaky now and then	Generally very good	Excellent
Do you have good control of your handwriting?	Sometimes it might get a little messy	My writing is mostly very clear	My writing is always neat
Are your sentences clear and coherent?	They sometimes run on too long	Mostly clear with only occasional lapses	Always clear without ambiguity
Do you have reasonable pace in your writing?	Sometimes I include too much detail	Mostly, but I can get sidetracked	Yes, I try to maintain a line of argument throughout

Sense of purpose

This relates to how well your writing adheres to the purpose of the task, including whether you have used an appropriate form and style of writing.

Upgrade

WRITING WITH PURPOSE	B	→ A	→ A*
Do you answer the questions directly?	Most of the time, although I sometimes go off topic	I'm always focused but I sometimes repeat points	My writing is always focused and progressive
Do you write with a reasonably academic style?	I write clearly but I could use better words and my writing sometimes lacks authority	I sometimes spend too long explaining the same point	My writing has authority and is also persuasive
Are you able to explain a point with efficiency and clarity?	I sometimes struggle to put complex ideas into words	Mostly clear with only occasional lapses	I make a point and move on, selecting the best words to express my ideas quickly and clearly
Do you show good judgement in terms of supporting points with evidence from the text?	I sometimes include quotations that are unnecessary or miss a chance to make a point about a piece of evidence	I sometimes get a little bogged-down with quotation and it can interrupt the flow of my argument	I use different methods to best support the point I wish to make, including use of short quotations and paraphrasing

Key words

Coverage – When responding to extract questions, aim to cover the whole extract selectively. When writing an essay about the whole text, choose parts of the novel that are the most relevant and revealing with regards to the question.

Organization of information

This relates to how well you construct your writing so that your points are grouped effectively and flow logically. This is primarily linked to how well you can use paragraphs to organize your ideas.

Upgrade

ORGANIZING YOUR WRITING	B	➡ A	➡ A*
Do you effectively group related points together in your essays?	Not always, I tend to write down my ideas as they come into my head so I don't always have time to group them	I try to but I might have to go over things I've already covered to include points that I've missed	Yes, I try to think ahead as I write so that I can link related points and build a progressive argument
Is there logical sequencing in how you order your paragraphs?	I have a good sense of when to start a new paragraph but I don't always think about the overall structure of my essays	My essays are well structured and easy to follow but could be more persuasive	I carefully control the order and structure of my paragraphs to strengthen my line of argument
Are there connections within each paragraph to keep your essay focused on the question?	Sometimes my paragraphs can run on too much and lose some of their focus	My paragraphs are mostly focused but I can get occasionally sidetracked	Yes, I ensure that every point I make is in some way linked to the question
Are you able to conclude your essays effectively?	Sometimes I struggle to wrap things up efficiently	I feel like I can spend too long trying to draw my writing to a close	I always try to think ahead to my final paragraph, so I know where I am heading as I write my essay

Question types

Extract questions

In your exam for Unit 1 and your exam for Unit 2, the first question that you will answer on your set novel will be an extract question. Extract questions provide a sharp twenty-minute challenge on a 'page' of text from your novel. You cannot predict which extract is going to be used, but you should be able to recognize it and work with it.

Critical to the success of your response to the extract will be your **focus** and your **coverage**.

Key words

Focus – Make sure your writing always relates to the task set and has a clear sense of purpose and progression.

Read the extract with a pen in your hand, and annotate it quickly, with your answer to the question in mind. Use underlining, arrows, asterisks and any other markings that will help you to refer back to ideas when you come to write your answer. Do all this at a quick pace, ideally taking no longer than five minutes.

When you write your answer, make sure you cover the extract in a balanced way.

> **➜ CHALLENGE**
>
> Select a page from the novel you are studying where a new character is introduced to the reader for the first time. Answer the following question with close reference to this extract:
>
> **How does the writer influence the reader's attitude in the extract?**

Essay questions

Following the extract question, you will be given a choice of two further questions on your set text. You must answer one of these. Both questions will relate to the whole text and at least one will be an essay-style question.

When writing a response to an essay-style question, remember to do the task as set. Start with an important point and give the examiner something positive to tick in the first sentence. Make the examiner think, 'High mark?' after the first paragraph. Mention the writer early on in your essay and see the writer as a crucial part of the discussion. Show enthusiasm and respect for each text and build your personal response into your answer.

> **Avoid**
>
> Don't allow your meaning and quality of expression to deteriorate under pressure in the exam.

> **➜ CHALLENGE**
>
> Write an opening to an essay in response to one of the following questions:
> * How is the theme of conflict presented in the novel?
> * How is the theme of friendship presented in the novel?
> * Choose one of the settings from your text and show how important it is to the novel as a whole.

Echo, or refer back to, the question in every paragraph. Often, one word will do it. If none of your paragraph ties in with the question, then you have drifted away. If so, don't panic, but return to the trail promptly. Use language to modify or clarify your meaning, as you proceed, rather than crossing out words and phrases. Crossings out show indecision, while skilful manoeuvring will reflect well on you.

The key unit of meaning is the sentence – ensure these are controlled and purposeful. Paragraphs are also important. No or few paragraphs can reveal problems with the authority and control of an argument. Use a paragraph for a definite purpose, such as discussing a specific point. End your response neatly without rambling.

Empathy questions

You may have the option of responding to a question that asks you to imagine you are a specific character from your text. This type of question is often referred to as an 'empathy question'. When responding to this type of question, you must 'put yourself in the shoes' of the character and write from his or her perspective, using words and phrases that he or she might use. Refer to events or conversations that that character participated in but try not to refer to any events that the character would not be aware of.

Read the extracts from two student responses that follow. Both were written in response to the exam question below:

Imagine you are one of the main characters. At the end of the story you look back at events. Write what you would say.

George – Of Mice and Men
I often got fed up of Lennie but I loved him. I always got frustrated at him when he was so forgetful, I hadda repeat myself several times, and Lennie always being so apologetic all the time. Though Lennie, he listened to me and he did remember 'the dream'. That was one thing he would never forget. The rabbits and to live off the 'fatta the lan'...

→ CHALLENGE

1. Discuss the qualities of reflection in the short sample answer above. How does the student achieve the right tone?
2. Which aspects, below, would help to make a top-grade response to an 'empathy' question? Discuss your ideas with a partner.
   - Sound knowledge of the text.
   - Accurate spelling, punctuation and grammar.
   - Reference to the five senses.
   - A convincing and sustained 'voice' that matches your character.
   - Selective references to events and other characters in the novel.
   - At least ten similes or metaphors.

→ **CHALLENGE**

Read the second sample student answer below. How does this student achieve the right tone? How convincing is this short piece of writing?

Atticus – To Kill a Mockingbird
It could perhaps be said that racism is socially accepted in Maycomb County and this is the main reason why Tom was convicted. Although many people didn't agree with my actions I just wouldn't have been able to hold my head up high on the streets if I had not defended an innocent man, despised because of the colour of his skin…

Both responses show how each student has attempted to reflect the character's views and attitudes in their writing, as well as the character's voice. To reach the higher grades with this type of response, you need to show implicit knowledge of the text, but also that you have taken on board the key themes and issues with which the characters are connected. You should also pay close attention to the wording of the question to ensure that your writing remains focused.

Demonstrating high-level skills

The student response on page 47 is based on the novel *Paddy Clarke Ha Ha Ha* by Roddy Doyle. The novel tells of growing up, friendship and family life from the perspective of a ten-year-old boy.

Read the essay question below and the response with comments from the examiner.

> How does Roddy Doyle portray Paddy 'growing up' in *Paddy Clarke Ha Ha Ha*?

This student jumps straight in with a valid point of focus. Charles Leavy is a minor character in some respects, but one with a pivotal role in Paddy's story.

The writing here is engaged, if a little disorganized, perhaps reflecting the pressure of the exam.

Good use of quotation. These quotations do not feel heavily rehearsed. They fit well into the answer without halting the flow of the writing.

The candidate is thinking on his/her feet. This essay lacks a little fluency and cohesion, but the points in this paragraph are apt and well expressed.

Good choice of language here ('wrenches') helps the student to add weight to this point.

A confident conclusion. The student concludes the essay with the end of the book, but also links it to the start of the book to make a shrewd point.

Growing up in Paddy Clarke Ha Ha Ha

One contribution to Paddy's growing up is his recent friendship with Charles Leavy. Paddy admires Charles and uses him to learn how to shut himself away from the reality of his domestic life. He does this by swearing, smacking and hurting his friends in the same way his father hurts his mother. When Kevin appeared on the scene in the school yard, he disowns him and turns into the bully. You get a look into Paddy's head by his actions. He is the victim who has turned into the bully. At other times Paddy attempts to build up defences and exclude himself from his parents' fights, "They were both to blame... It didn't take three; there was no room for me."

Paddy thinks he is growing up, but of course doesn't know as much as he thinks he knows. He does not understand the reason for the arguments between his parents, "Why didn't Da like Ma? – What was wrong with her?" Paddy turns to Sinbad for comfort, but his younger brother has already developed a method of "shutting himself from the world" and this makes Paddy jealous.

Another catalyst is Paddy's fight with Kevin, his former best friend. This marks a turning point in Paddy's life and he can recognize this, "It would never go back to the same again". As a result of this fight, Paddy is "boycotted" and becomes the outsider he has recently longed to be.

The final incident which wrenches Paddy from his childhood is when he witnesses his father hitting his mother. This converts all of Paddy's love and care for his father into hatred, "he looked at me. He unmade his fist." Paddy thinks of his parent as "He", which is cold and impersonal. Paddy remains calm, and this alone suggests adultness.

The meeting with his father on Christmas Eve is formal and Paddy's words are stilted, "How are you? – Very well, thank you." Paddy knows that he will never feel the same way about his father and has accepted his faults and violent, unpredictable temper. At the start of the book, there is a scene where Paddy's Da behaves like a father, looking at things through a magnifying glass with his son. At that point they were close. Now the barriers are up, and this last episode in the story suggests how far Paddy has come, even though he is still a child.

This answer also recognizes a wider conundrum in the text; that is the contradiction of a ten-year-old boy 'growing up'.

This response is very perceptive and also agile in terms of the way the student is able to select evidence from different parts of the novel to support his/her points. As well as dealing with the detail of specific events in the novel, the answer also reaches out to consider wider issues, such as the notion of childhood and what differentiates an 'adult' perspective from a 'childish' one. With the addition of a few more developed paragraphs, this response is well on the way to securing an A* grade.

Final word

What makes a high-level response to prose?

To achieve the highest grades, you need to be prepared to read the texts you are studying in full, in your own time as well as in class. When you read, read with a questioning attitude – identifying issues and topics worth talking about. Be confident in forming your own judgements about characters, themes and events and support your ideas by ranging widely across the text.

You will need to have a good working knowledge of the plot for each novel you are studying, but you will not gain any great credit for writing it down in the exam. Your knowledge of the general outline of the story and your more detailed knowledge of characters and events must underpin a deeper analysis.

Further task

For each set prose text that you study, you will have **one hour** of exam time to answer two questions. The first question (part (i)) will be based on an extract from the text. You will then be given a choice of two questions on the novel as a whole and you should answer <u>either</u> part (ii) <u>or</u> part (iii).

In the real exam, the extract will be printed on the exam paper but for this practice activity you will need to select a page from your text to focus on. Try to complete the tasks as if you were sitting them in the exam. You should spend 20 minutes on part (i) and about 40 minutes on part (ii) or part (iii).

Once you have finished your response to both questions, use the **Upgrade** assessment criteria on page 49 to grade your work. Use the criteria to determine what you need to do to improve and write down three changes that could help you to boost your answer into the next grade band, or allow you to secure a stronger A*.

---

*Answer part (i) and **either** part (ii) **or** part (iii).*

(i) Read the last full page of your chosen novel. Then answer the following question:

     With close reference to the extract, show how the writer creates mood and atmosphere here.   [10]

Either,

(ii) How effective is the ending of the novel you have studied?   [20+4]

    Marks for spelling, punctuation and the accurate use of grammar will be allocated to this question in your Unit 2 examination.

Or,

(iii) Imagine you are one of the main characters at the start of the novel. Describe your hopes and fears.   [20+4]

    Marks for spelling, punctuation and the accurate use of grammar will be allocated to this question in your Unit 2 examination.

Use the marking criteria below to assess your answer to the
practice task on page 48. Decide how you could improve your
work to help push your answer into the next grade band.

Critical response

1. Does the response show a consistent understanding of the text and the ability to move from the specific to the general?
2. Does the response include perceptive and insightful comments about characters, relationships and settings, showing links to wider themes?
3. Does the response successfully evaluate the attitudes and motives presented in the text?
4. Does the response convey ideas persuasively and use well-selected evidence?

Language, structure, form

1. Does the response show appreciation of how writers use language to achieve specific effects?
2. Does the response evaluate how the structure of the novel influences the meaning?

Reference to contexts

1. Does the response make insightful points about the text, using specific contextual knowledge?
2. Does the response make revealing points about the text by relating it to personal experiences and to the experiences of others?

A*

Critical response

1. Does the response show appreciation of the text as a whole as well as focusing on the detail?
2. Does the response make relevant comments about characters, relationships and settings, making reference to wider themes?
3. Does the response explore the attitudes and motives of the writer as presented in the text?
4. Is evidence well selected, clear and appropriate?

Language, structure, form

1. Does the response show understanding of how writers use language to achieve effects?
2. Does the response make insightful points about how the structure of the novel influences the meaning of the text?

Reference to contexts

1. Does the response make specific contextual points in order to highlight meaning in the text?
2. Does the response offer insight into the text by relating it to personal experiences and the experiences of others?

A

Critical response

1. Does the response show comfortable understanding of the text?
2. Does the response comment on characters, relationships, themes and settings?
3. Does the response consider the attitudes and motives of the writer as presented in the text?
4. Does the response include relevant evidence?

Language, structure, form

1. Does the response discuss how the writer uses language to achieve effects?
2. Does the response consider how the structure of the novel influences the meaning of the text?
3. Does the response consider the effects of stylistic features?

Reference to contexts

1. Does the response acknowledge the importance of specific contexts when reading and interpreting the text?
2. Does the response show the ability to relate the text to personal experiences and the experiences of others?

B

Aim for A

- You can write a purposeful response to the question set.
- You have a clear grasp of the characters and the plot.
- You have a confident understanding of the whole text as well as the ability to select and comment on appropriate details.
- You have a secure appreciation of the background to texts and a clear sense of the genre.

Aim for A*

- You can produce a tightly argued essay with some individuality and style.
- You can demonstrate an impressive understanding of character and plot.
- You can select evidence from across the text to best support your argument and your ideas about the text as a whole.
- Your contextual understanding is well judged and integrated into your essay.

Studying drama

How does the study of drama differ from the study of prose? There are inevitably similarities but some important differences too. Prose and drama both have characters, relationships and dialogue. They also both have plot, setting and mood and atmosphere. Like novels, drama texts confront issues and explore themes.

However, you should always bear in mind that a drama script is intended for the stage, where actors make it come alive. Learning in the classroom can unintentionally confuse the genres of prose and drama. For example, you might read out parts of a novel in class, as you might a play. Ironically, classes often read plays while seated at their desks, which can make it easy to overlook how it might appear when acted out in an open space.

For your GCSE English Literature qualification, you have to study **one** drama text for examination. You will <u>not</u> be able to take a copy of the play into the examinations with you.

→ CHALLENGE

Consider the play you are studying – list ten things that are likely to be lost in a static, seated classroom reading.

▶ THE ASSESSMENT

GCSE English Literature Unit 2 Section 1

In Section 1 of your **exam** for Unit 2, you will be assessed on **either** a contemporary drama text **or** a literary heritage drama text. Section 2 of this exam focuses on the study of a prose text, which is covered in Chapter 2 of the book.

You will have two hours to complete the entire exam paper for Unit 2, which means you should allow **one hour** to complete the section dealing with the drama text that you have studied.

In the exam you will have to answer **two** questions on the play. The first question (**part (i)**) will require close reading of an extract. You should spend 20 minutes on this question. The second question will offer a choice of tasks (**part (ii) or part (iii)**) and both will relate to the text as a whole. You should spend 40 minutes on this second question.

Your ability to spell, punctuate and use grammar accurately will be assessed in your answer to either question (ii) or question (iii).

→ CHALLENGE

Consider the play you are studying. What is the overall balance between the dialogue and the action? Do the words dominate, or does the action? How important is language in the play and, on the other hand, how 'theatrical' is it?

Conflict and tension

There can be plenty of conflict and tension in novels, but these things form the very lifeblood of plays. In *Blood Brothers,* the following exchanges are significant in terms of the development of the plot, but what happens here is enough to make even a casual onlooker feel on edge.

> **Avoid**
>
> Don't lose sight of the fact that plays are different from novels.

→ CHALLENGE

The short extracts, below, are only moments apart in the same scene. How does the writer succeed in making the situation escalate in such a short span of time?

Blood Brothers

Mrs Lyons:	Oh Richard, Richard.
Mr Lyons:	For God's sake, Jennifer, I told you on the phone, he'll just be out playing somewhere.
Mrs Lyons:	But where?
Mr Lyons:	Outside somewhere, with friends. Edward…
Mrs Lyons:	But I don't want him out playing.
Mr Lyons:	Jennifer, he's not a baby.
Mrs Lyons:	I don't care. I don't care…
Mr Lyons:	For Christ's sake, you bring me home from work in the middle of the day, just to say you haven't seen him for an hour. Perhaps we should be talking about you getting something for your nerves…

…He turns to look at her but she looks away. He sighs and absently bends to pick up a pair of children's shoes from the floor.

Mr Lyons:	I really do think you should see a doctor.
Mrs Lyons:	*(snapping)* I don't need to see a doctor. I just need to move away from this neighbourhood, because I'm frightened. I'm frightened for Edward.
Mr Lyons:	*(places the shoes on the table before turning on her.)* Frightened of what, woman?
Mrs Lyons:	*(wheeling to face him):* Frightened of… *(She is stopped by the sight of the shoes on the table. She rushes at the table and sweeps the shoes off.)*

Willy Russell

Whenever you read a piece of drama, try to get into the habit of asking questions about how the play might work on the stage or screen. Discuss your ideas with the rest of the class. The scene from *Blood Brothers* has a direct impact on the audience by building up tension. Identifying this effect and recognizing how it is achieved are vital in terms of interpreting the scene and the writer's intentions.

Understanding stage directions

Stage directions in many plays show the playwright's specific intentions in terms of the presentation and development of key characters. At the start of *An Inspector Calls*, for example, the Inspector enters for the first time and the playwright is keen that this entrance makes an impact. The Inspector orchestrates the action in the play and is present throughout. He is real enough. The playwright wants his presence to be unambiguous, not a Shakespearean ghost but an Inspector Goole.

An Inspector Calls

Edna: *(opening door, and announcing)*
Inspector Goole.
*The Inspector enters, and **Edna**
goes, closing door after her. The
Inspector need not be a big
man but he creates at once an
impression of massiveness, solidity
and purposefulness. He is a man
in his fifties, dressed in a plain
darkish suit of the period. He
speaks carefully, weightily, and has
a disconcerting habit of looking hard
at the person he addresses before
actually speaking.*

J. B. Priestley

→ CHALLENGE

1. How do the stage directions above make you view the Inspector?
2. Are characters less well developed in plays than novels? Discuss your thoughts with a partner and compare your views.

Dramatic irony

Dramatic irony is the playwright's technique for revealing something of significance to the audience that cannot be seen by a key character. In other words, you get it and the character does not. In Shakespeare, this can seem incredibly obvious and yet the characters still do not catch on!

Othello is a play about jealousy, racism and evil intent. More interestingly, it is also a play about trickery and deception, being deceived and deceiving others.

In a soliloquy in Act 1 Scene 3, Iago says that he hates Othello. Othello is not there to hear it; the audience is. Later in the play, in Act 3 Scene 3, Iago swears to Othello that he will do everything he can to help Othello seek revenge on those he mistrusts. Othello trusts Iago's word and there you have dramatic irony. The rest is tragedy!

→ CHALLENGE

1. What effect does the use of dramatic irony have on the way you feel about Iago?
2. How is this likely to influence your overall experience of the play?

Othello

Iago: I hate the Moor…
[…]
The Moor is of a free and open nature,
That thinks men honest that but seem to be so,
And will as tenderly be led by the nose
As asses are.

Othello: *[Kneels]*
In the due reverence of a sacred vow
I here engage my words.
Iago: Do not rise yet.
[He kneels]
Witness you ever-burning lights above,
You elements that clip us round about,
Witness that here Iago doth give up
The execution of his wit, hands, heart,
To wrong'd Othello's service. Let him command,
And to obey shall be in me remorse,
What bloody business ever.
[They rise]

William Shakespeare

Characters and relationships

Key words

Dialogue – The conversation of a play, that is, the words spoken by characters to each other and overheard by the audience.

Characters in drama are described in the playscript, but brought to life by the **dialogue** and the actors. Read two short extracts from *Hobson's Choice* by Harold Brighouse, below. Consider how the writer creates a strong sense of Willie Mossop's personality and character through a combination of dialogue and stage directions.

Hobson's Choice

Mrs. H: Who's Willie?

Hobson: Name of Mossop, madam. But if there is anything wrong I assure you I'm capable of making the man suffer for it. I'll –

Willie Mossop comes up trap. He is a lanky fellow, about thirty, not naturally stupid but stunted mentally by a brutalized childhood. He is a raw material of a charming man, but, at present, it requires a very keen eye to detect his potentialities. His clothes are an even poorer edition of Tubby's. He comes half-way up trap.

Willie: I'm not much good at talking, and I always seem to say wrong things when I do talk. I'm sorry if my well-meant words don't suit your taste, but I thought you came here for advice.

Hobson: I didn't come to you, you jumped-up cock-a-hooping – *(Rising.)*

Maggie: That'll do, father. *(Pushes him down.)* My husband's trying to help you.

Harold Brighouse

→ **CHALLENGE**

1. How does the dialogue support the description of Willie Mossop presented in the stage directions?
2. How is this likely to influence the way the audience reacts to Willie?

Characters and themes

Top-grade students will show the ability to weigh up characters. As well as understanding how they are presented to the audience, they will also offer a level of judgement, where they consider the significance of the character in connection with the writer's intentions and important **themes** in the play.

Read the extracts below from two student answers. The first focuses on the presentation of Mrs Birling in *An Inspector Calls*. Mrs Birling is the upper-class wife of self-interested businessman Mr Birling. The second response considers the significance of Linda in *Blood Brothers*, a woman whose loyalty to the man she loves is tested by his immutable depression and spiralling drug addiction.

As you read each response, consider how each student successfully links the character they are focusing on to other characters in the play. Both students attempt to evaluate the impact of the character's actions and make judgements about how the character is significant in terms of the overall plot and wider themes.

→ CHALLENGE

1. Use the **Upgrade** panel on page 57 to rate each student's performance.
2. How could each answer be improved? Discuss your ideas with a partner.

<u>How does the playwright present the character of Mrs Birling to the audience?</u>

Mrs Birling, like her husband, abused her power, authority and influence to ensure that Eva Smith was not helped by the Brumley Women's Charity Organization. She admits herself as being 'prejudiced against her case' because Eva called herself 'Mrs Birling'. Mrs Birling felt this was a deliberate sign of 'gross impertinence' and insolence. Yet, despite Eva's death, she still felt no remorse or compassion.

Mrs Birling defends her decision before the Inspector, stating 'Yes, it was' her influence, as a prominent member of the community, that finally refused to give Eva Smith any help, insisting that Eva Smith simply did not make the right claims. Mrs Birling intimates that Eva was a liar and disrespectful and thus justifies her decision to have the claim refused.

<u>How important is Linda to the play as a whole?</u>

When the audience see Linda hand Mickey the pills, we know that she has once again given in to Mickey because she undeniably loves him and can't bear to see him suffer or depressed. This highlights the softness in Linda's character, portraying her sympathetic side to the spectators.

'Could I talk to Councillor Lyons, please?' – This line foreshadows the tragic outcome of the storyline as it ultimately leads on to the affair between Eddie and Linda. The audience feel that this is wrong (knowing the future), however, they can really understand Linda's desperation for some love and comfort as she is receiving none at home with Mickey.

All of this makes Linda a very important character within the play. A pattern throughout Mickey's life is that he has always wanted what Eddie has. The only 'possession' which was truly earned and therefore his 'own' was Linda. This is because ultimately Mickey's whole existence is built upon everything Eddie has given him. So when Mickey realizes he has now even lost Linda to Eddie who already has everything he craves he is heartbroken; his anger, jealousy, bitterness and sadness at losing his beloved drives him to end Eddie's life and his own. The character of Linda is the catalyst that determines the outcome of the tragic plot.

Upgrade

A* ↑	The answer shows a strong grasp of the text as a whole but also focuses on precise details that help to support points. The answer judges the significance of key characters and events within the play, as well as indentifying how these are presented to the audience. The answer considers the writer's attitude and also how events and characters link to wider themes or messages in the text.
A ↑	The answer shows a good grasp of the text as a whole and also relates to relevant detail in the text. The answer considers the significance of key characters and events within the play, as well as showing how these are presented to the audience. The answer touches on how characters and events might relate to wider themes.
B	The answer makes reference to relevant events in the text to help support points about characters. The answer makes valid points about how the writer presents characters to the audience.

→ CHALLENGE

Choose one of the questions attempted by the students and apply it to a character in the play you are studying. Write the first three paragraphs of a response to the question.

Writing about style and structure

Style in drama

In prose, style is associated with the narrator and directly with the words on the page; in drama, you can concentrate on setting, performance, **dramatic effects** and dramatic signals.

The whole of *A View from the Bridge,* by Arthur Miller, takes place in, or next to, a New York tenement building. It is meant to be a claustrophobic setting and this creates an increasingly tense atmosphere. The overcrowded living conditions are present on stage and also in the words and actions of the characters as a tragic situation unfolds. Call it style or call it stagecraft, it is the playwright initially and then the director and actors who are responsible for the effectiveness of the drama.

Key words

Dramatic effects
– This includes anything which happens during a play to produce a response in members of the audience.

> **→ CHALLENGE**
>
> Discuss in detail the shape of the play you are studying, in terms of any of the following:
> * locations
> * dramatic techniques employed by the playwright
> * any dramatic moments that stand out as memorable.

The structure of a play

Like novels, plays can have particular structural features that stand out to the audience or help to lend emphasis to a certain character, theme or the overall impact of the play. For example, *A View from the Bridge* begins and ends with Alfieri commenting on the action. As you study your drama text, be alert to the parallels, the sub-plots, the ironies, and the causes and outcomes that affect the characters.

Pay close attention to **exits and entrances** in the play and how frequently specific characters appear on stage, in which settings and whether alone or with others. This is all part of the structure of the drama and a deliberate means by which the playwright shapes the action.

Key words

Exits and entrances
– These are very significant in a play, because scenes change when someone leaves and someone else arrives. You see the characters in different situations.

> **→ CHALLENGE**
>
> What can you say about the structure of the play you are studying with regards to each of the points below?
> * The opening and the ending
> * Climactic events or turning points in the play
> * Running or recurring themes.

Comic resolutions

Comedies have specific structural characteristics – most notably, perhaps, in the sense that they offer a happy ending. They move from disorder to order, and from chaos to harmony. At the end of Shakespeare's *Much Ado about Nothing*, for example, everything is tied up neatly with marriage.

> **→ CHALLENGE**
>
> Consider the play you are studying. How well does the ending fit with the overall tone of the play? Is the ending tragic and distressing or does it bring a fulfilling sense of resolution to the play?

You will note the potential for comedy to enclose darker, even disturbing undertones, which may impact on how fulfilling the outcome really is. The **director** and the actors will have some influence over how these elements are treated and how they are presented to the audience.

> **→ CHALLENGE**
>
> Consider the play you are studying. Are there any characters or events that could be presented in different ways? Discuss your ideas with a partner.

Key words

Director – A director supervises and instructs actors who are appearing in the production of a play.

Avoid ⚠

Do not 'offload' paragraphs of historical information in the exam. This will not gain you any marks!

Understanding the background to texts

Sensitivity to important social, historical and cultural contexts is an integral feature of a good-quality answer, but to be effective your comments <u>must</u> be connected to your interpretation of the meaning of the text. Similarly, discussions about characters and relationships need to be rooted in the circumstances and messages of the play; otherwise appreciation of the play as a work of literature will become lost in favour of retelling of the story.

The lives of ordinary people are the focus of many contemporary plays. *My Mother Said I Never Should,* by Charlotte Keatley, portrays four generations of family across the breadth of the 20th century. The play deals with ordinary people, their hopes, struggles, celebrations and disappointments. *Be My Baby*, by Amanda Whittington, looks back at the tough life for a young expectant mother in the 1960s. In exploring the experiences of these characters, both plays tackle a range of wider social issues.

This is also the case for heritage plays. The action of the play may take place in a historical setting but it is likely to deal with themes and concerns that echo those of our own times. When writing about *An Inspector Calls*, you would have a golden opportunity to probe the issue of social responsibility in Britain well beyond the Birling family. Whatever your text, do not miss an opportunity to look outwards to connected, wider issues. However, remember to always return to the text and remain focused on the task.

→ **CHALLENGE**

1. In groups, do a small amount of research around the play you are studying in terms of the following:
   - the age in which the play was written
   - the social values of the time
   - the experiences and intentions of the playwright.
2. For each topic, present two or three concise points to the rest of the class, linking each point to a specific observation about the play.

Question types

Your exam on your set drama text will take the same format as your exams on the novels you have studied. Your first question, (part (i)), will be an extract-based question. You will then choose your second question from two possible options (part (ii)) or (part (iii)). Similarly, as is the case for the prose text you have studied, your answer to either part (ii) or part (iii) will also be assessed according to the accuracy of your spelling, punctuation and grammar. The questions may consist of an essay-based question, an 'empathy' question or possibly a director-style question. The first three question types are covered in Chapter 2. The director-style question is outlined below.

Answering questions on being a director

This type of question asks you to imagine that you are the director giving advice to an actor about how to perform the role of a particular character in the play.

All drama comes to life on stage and screen. A question involving directors and actors reminds us of that. There is nothing outlandish about this type of question, so you should still set out to show your understanding of the play and your ability to select relevant detail. You will consider the plot, characters, relationships, language and meaning, just the same as usual. Answer the question and use evidence from the text to support your suggestions. Do not dumb down your approach by fussing about costume and make-up. At the heart of a director-style question is a question about characters.

→ **CHALLENGE**

Plan a response to the practice exam question below, based on your set play.

Imagine you are giving advice to someone who is going to take the part of one of the characters in the play. Tell him/her how he/she should present the character to the audience. If you wish, you may focus on specific parts of the play.

Demonstrating high-level skills

The following high-grade student response is based on the play *An Inspector Calls* by J. B. Priestley. Read the response and comments from the examiner, which show why this answer achieved high marks.

Gentle, rather slow-paced opening – but focuses immediately on the task.

The student quickly prioritizes Mr Birling for detailed consideration.

Short paragraphs help to keep the writing tight and to the point.

A confident judgement of Mr Birling conveyed with feeling.

Continuing very strongly with crisp points about key characters.

Some judgement in terms of apportioning blame but perhaps more could be said to justify this point.

Good attention to detail, and all the time evaluating events rather than simply retelling the plot.

An impressive conclusion that draws each thread of the essay together while also looking outwards to consider wider 'messages' in the play.

What do you think are the most important factors that contributed to Eva Smith's death?

There are several important factors that contributed to Eva Smith's death – the actions and behaviour of Mr and Mrs Birling and the relationship with Gerald and with Eric. It is the accumulation of these various factors which, I believe, drove Eva Smith to take her own life.

Mr Birling is a bumptious, conceited and a 'hard-headed business man'. His primary concern is therefore his business, and his wealth. All his speeches in Act One, whilst beginning with the expression of his happiness for his daughter's engagement, ended with discussion of business and 'prosperity'.

The Inspector prompts Birling to admit his involvement with Eva Smith. He had employed her nearly two years before her death. However, he sacked her from her position because she had the audacity to ask for an increase in pay. Mr Birling 'refused, of course'. Eva Smith disrespectfully opposed Mr Birling, 'She'd had a lot to say – far too much – so she had to go'.

Birling's blinkered and dogmatic beliefs and his greed for money contributed to the death of Eva Smith as he used his power – his authority and class and wealth – to force Eva Smith to leave, making her redundant and unable to provide for herself.

Mrs Birling, like her husband, is also guilty of abusing her power and influence over Eva. Eva goes to her for help but she is refused it. Even after Eva's death, Mrs Birling shows how cold and callous she is by continuing to imply that Eva was a liar and disrespectful and that she therefore deserved the treatment she received. Sheila, however, though she played a significant part in contributing to Eva's death, cannot be condemned as much as her parents. Sheila confesses she got Eva Smith sacked from Milward's because she was jealous of her beauty and used her influence to ensure she was made redundant: 'I told him that if they didn't get rid of that girl, I'd never go near the place again… I'd persuade mother to close our account with them.'

Gerald Croft claims that he didn't 'Install her (Eva Smith) there so that I could make love to her' but in order to help her. He rescued her from the advances of a local drunk, Joe Meggarty, and gave her food, shelter and stability. However, however unintentionally, he ended the affair badly and abruptly and this inevitably made Eva Smith feel used and manipulated.

To make matters worse, Eric became involved with her also and made her pregnant, but she ended the relationship although he offered her money. She then turned to Mrs Birling for help.

It is quite evident that although each of the characters were linked to Eva Smith, like rings on a chain, no one knew about the other. Each character betrayed Eva Smith morally – they each manipulated Eva's lack of authority and low social class. Mr and Mrs Birling used social politics to justify their actions. These blinkered views of class and lack of responsibility were apparent in each relationship. This is the most important factor which contributed to Eva Smith's death – the lack of responsibility for one's own actions – but also the lack of community. The lack of compassion and human decency to help someone in trouble, asking for nothing in return.

Final word

What makes a high-grade response to drama?

A top student, when writing about a play, will be comfortable exploring the potential of the drama beyond the words spoken by the characters. He or she will be able to write sensitively, understanding the writer's intentions and appreciating the subtleties of the language. There will be some appreciation of the historical and theatrical context of the play but this will not distract from a purposeful consideration of the text.

Further task

Complete the practice exam questions below as if you were sitting the real exam. You should spend 20 minutes on part (i) and about 40 minutes on <u>either</u> part (ii) <u>or</u> part (iii).

In the real exam, the extract will be printed on the exam paper, but for the purposes of this practice task, you will need to select a page from your text to focus on.

Once you have finished your response to both questions, use the **Upgrade** assessment criteria on page 63 to grade your work. Use the criteria to determine what you need to do to improve and write down three changes that could help you to boost your answer into the next grade band, or allow you to secure a stronger A*.

Answer part (i) and **either** *part (ii)* **or** *part (iii).*

(i) Choose an extract that represents a turning point in the play. Then answer the following question:

With close reference to the extract, show how the playwright makes this scene dramatic.   [10]

Either,

(ii) How important is conflict in the play as a whole?   [20+4]

Marks for spelling, punctuation and the accurate use of grammar are allocated to this question.

Or,

(iii) Imagine you are one of the main characters at the end of the play. Describe your feelings looking back over what you have experienced.
                                                              [20+4]

Marks for spelling, punctuation and the accurate use of grammar are allocated to this question.

Use the marking criteria below to assess your answer to the practice task on page 62. Decide how you could improve your work to help push your answer into the next grade band.

A*

Critical response

1. Does the response show a consistent understanding of the text and the ability to move from the specific to the general?
2. Does the response include perceptive and insightful comments about characters, relationships and events, showing links to wider themes?
3. Does the response successfully evaluate the attitudes and motives as presented in the text?
4. Does the response convey ideas persuasively and use well-selected evidence?

Language, structure, form

1. Does the response show appreciation of how writers use language and dramatic features to achieve specific effects?
2. Does the response evaluate how the structure of the play influences the meaning?

Reference to contexts

1. Does the response successfully identify the text as drama and show appreciation of how audiences receive and relate to this genre?
2. Does the response make revealing points about the text by relating it to context, personal experiences and the experiences of others?

A

Critical response

1. Does the response show appreciation of the text as a whole as well as focusing on the detail?
2. Does the response make relevant comments about characters, relationships and events, making reference to wider themes?
3. Does the response explore the attitudes and motives of the writer as presented in the text?
4. Is evidence well-selected, clear and appropriate?

Language, structure, form

1. Does the response show understanding of how writers use language to achieve effects?
2. Does the response make insightful points about how the structure of the play influences the meaning of the text?

Reference to contexts

1. Does the response acknowledge the text as drama and show awareness of how audiences receive and relate to this genre?
2. Does the response offer insight into the text by relating it to context, personal experiences and the experiences of others?

B

Critical response

1. Does the response show comfortable understanding of the text?
2. Does the response comment on characters, relationships, themes and events?
3. Does the response consider the attitudes and motives of the writer as presented in the text?
4. Does the response include relevant evidence?

Language, structure, form

1. Does the response discuss how the writer uses language to achieve effects?
2. Does the response consider how the structure of the play influences the meaning of the text?

Reference to contexts

1. Does the response show some awareness of how audiences receive and relate to drama?
2. Does the response relate the text to context and personal experiences?

Chapter 4   Literary Heritage Poetry and Shakespeare

Aim for A

- You can write a confident, fluent and thorough essay response.
- You can present a purposeful response to the question, identifying relevant links between the texts.
- You can achieve a good balance in terms of your coverage of the Shakespeare play and the poems.
- You can move comfortably from the detail of the texts to an overview.

Aim for A*

- Your essay will be well structured, with a clear thematic thread that runs cohesively through the essay.
- Your writing will include evidence of integrated and well-judged contextual understanding, with well-developed links.
- You can move from detail to overview with skill, covering each of the texts in a balanced way.
- Your essay will be tightly argued, with some individuality and style.

Studying heritage poetry with Shakespeare

For this part of your course, you will study literary heritage poems from a collection set by the exam board. This collection spans time from the 16th century to the present day. It includes some great poets and some great poems. It also includes some lesser known poets. With 64 poems across the ages, there is certainly plenty to read and talk about!

In addition to the poetry, you will also study a play by Shakespeare. Your teacher will suggest a suitable play to study. This may be any Shakespeare play, with the exception of *Othello* or *Much Ado about Nothing*, which are possible choices for your exam in Unit 2. Whatever play you are studying, try to read the play in full. You should also try to see the play in performance, if possible.

THE ASSESSMENT

GCSE English Literature Unit 3

You will study a Shakespeare play and a selection of Literary Heritage poetry for Unit 3 of your GCSE English Literature assessment. This will be examined by Controlled Assessment. The Controlled Assessment will last **four hours** in total and will probably be divided into two or more shorter sessions.

You will submit one extended piece of writing covering both the poetry and the Shakespeare play that you have studied. The texts chosen must be linked by a theme and you must write about the ways in which the thematic link is explored in the texts. Each year, the exam board will choose two themes from the list below. You will base your study on one of the topics suggested.

You are allowed to take in **one side of A4** containing your own notes but this must <u>not</u> contain a draft of your answer.

Avoid

Don't limit yourself to one fixed interpretation of a theme. Different writers may approach it in entirely different ways.

The themes

You will base your linked essay on a specific theme, exploring how this theme is treated in the poetry and the Shakespeare play and identifying links between the texts. The exam board will nominate two themes from the list each year:

- love
- family and parent–child relationships
- youth and age
- power and ambition
- male–female relationships and the role of women
- hypocrisy and prejudice
- conflict
- grief.

Understanding the task

The task below is an example of the type of essay you might be asked to write for your assessment.

> Many plays and poems are concerned with the relationship between men and women. Choose one relationship between a man and a woman in the drama you have studied and link it with similar relationships in the poetry you have studied.

The example task below shows how this question could be adapted to relate to the play and poems you are studying. There are three parts to this question – showing how you need to write about the Shakespeare play, the poems you have studied and also explore links between the texts.

- *Look at the way Shakespeare presents a key male–female relationship in the play you have studied. How does Shakespeare show the influence of one character over the other?*
- *Consider the way male–female relationships are presented in poems in the collection. Write about at least two poems in detail but make references to others.*
- *Explore the links between the poems and the Shakespeare play, developing your personal response to the texts. You may treat this as a separate, third part of the essay or integrate your links and views into the second part.*

→ CHALLENGE

1. Could the task above be adapted to relate to the Shakespeare play you are studying? If so, which characters and relationships would you focus on?
2. Identify possible poems from the heritage poetry collection that would provide interesting links to the same theme.

Studying Shakespeare

In your essay you can concentrate on particular scenes, but to achieve the highest grades you must be able to demonstrate knowledge and understanding of the whole play.

The following pages will not give you the 'answers' in terms of how to interpret your Shakespeare play – that is for you to decide! However, they do potentially offer an extra dimension in terms of thinking and writing about the play as well as forming **links** with the poetry.

Key words

Links – Any kind of connection between the texts, whether similarities, differences, parallels or crossovers. Keep a note of links you identify as you read and study the texts.

Comedy or tragedy

Shakespeare's plays are often defined in terms of **genre**. Tragedies typically involve themes such as violence, betrayal, loss and death. Comedies, on the other hand, tend to focus on love, marriage, friendship and potentially some form of confusion arising from mixed-up identity.

As well as comedies and tragedies, some of Shakespeare's plays get categorized as 'history plays'; others are hard to categorize. History plays deal with the life of a historical figure (often with tragic elements), whereas plays such as *The Merchant of Venice* and *The Winter's Tale* include a combination of comic and tragic elements. Characters often survive to see the end, but face serious risks along the way.

→ CHALLENGE

Discuss the play you are studying with a partner. Does it fit neatly into any of the categories described above? Why or why not?
Here is the list again:

- tragedies
- comedies
- history plays.

Chaos and order

Shakespeare's plays often demonstrate movement from chaos to order. This may be apparent in terms of the structure of the play – i.e. the sequence in which things happen. Or it may be apparent in the language characters use to describe what is happening around them.

Shakespeare's plays about kings and heroes inevitably deal with countries in strife, but also with leaders showing great character and human frailty. For Elizabethans, the monarch was second only to God and there was a genuine fear that, if the rightful person was removed from the throne, then the world would be plunged into chaos. There was also faith in the idea that the succession of a rightful monarch would naturally restore order. But who was ever truly rightful?

Shakespeare's play *Julius Caesar* deals directly with the disorder that ensues when a state loses its leader. Julius Caesar himself is dead by Act 3, having been assassinated by conspirators led by Brutus. However, Brutus is defeated and killed in the subsequent chaos by the forces of Mark Antony and Octavius Caesar. The play ends with Antony and Octavius seizing power.

→ **CHALLENGE**

Read the extract, below, taken from the end of *Julius Caesar*. Do these lines convey the sense that order has been restored or are you doubtful?

Julius Caesar

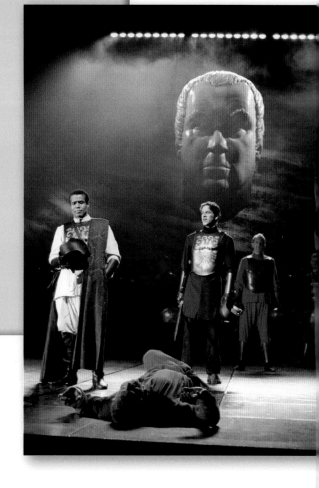

Antony: This was the noblest Roman of them all:
All the conspirators, save only he,
Did that they did in envy of great Caesar.
He only, in a general honest thought
And common good to all, made one of them.
His life was gentle, and the elements
So mix'd in him that Nature might stand up
And say to all the world, 'This was a man!'

Octavius: According to his virtue let us use him,
With all respect and rites of burial.
Within my tent his bones tonight shall lie,
Most like a soldier, order'd honourably.
So call the field to rest, and let's away
To part the glories of this happy day.

The tragic hero

What makes a tragic hero? Read what some other students had to say.

❝A tragic hero is someone who has everything to begin with but loses everything through making bad decisions.❞

❝It definitely has to be the main character. To be a hero, it has to be the person the audience focuses on the most.❞

❝It's a character who suffers greatly for something they want badly.❞

❝Tragic heroes stand out from others because of their extreme actions. They make drastic decisions and take risks.❞

→ **CHALLENGE**

1. Do you agree or disagree with the views on page 68? Is there anything else you would add? Do you think, for example, that tragic heroes are always to blame for their actions?
2. Why might some people have the opinion that the treacherous Macbeth is a tragic hero, but that the innocent Romeo and Juliet are not?

Comic resolutions

Key words

Convention – An aspect of style, character, plot or setting that is a common feature of a particular type of text, such as weddings at the end of comedies rather than deaths at the end of tragedies.

Elizabethan comedies end with the **convention** of wedding celebrations, which is also a means of re-establishing 'order'. This is identifiable in Shakespearean comedies. However, Shakespeare always liked to bend convention too, and sometimes leaves someone on the 'outside looking in'. Characters that are 'left out' in this way perhaps do not get the same sense of a 'happy ending'. As you study your play, think about things Shakespeare does to challenge expectations and conventions.

→ **CHALLENGE**

Answer the following questions about the play you are studying:
1. Does the play present a shift from order to disorder?
2. What is the cause of the disorder in the play?
3. To what extent is order restored at the end?

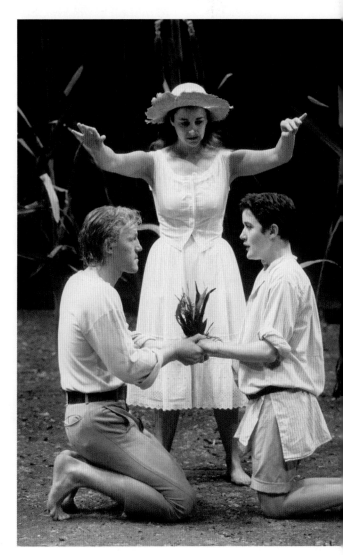

Appearance and reality

Key words

Dramatic irony – A dramatic effect created when the audience knows more about what's going on onstage than the characters do.

Things are not always what they seem in Shakespeare's plays. Disguise and deception frequently feature in the comedies as well as the tragedies. Disguise is often a key feature of the plot, for example, where characters pose as other characters to deceive or outwit others. This often works on the basis of **dramatic irony** in that the audience always knows who is who, while the characters do not.

In Shakespeare's comedy *Twelfth Night*, Viola disguises herself as a man in order to find work at Duke Orsino's court. However, Viola soon falls in love with the Duke, which puts her in a difficult predicament, considering Orsino believes she is a man.

Read the extract from *Twelfth Night*, below, and think about how Shakespeare makes this dilemma entertaining for the audience.

Twelfth Night

Orsino: There is no woman's sides
Can bide the beating of so strong a passion
As love doth give my heart; no woman's heart
So big, to hold so much. They lack retention.
Alas, their love may be call'd appetite,
No motion of the liver, but the palate,
That suffers surfeit, cloyment, and revolt;
But mine is all as hungry as the sea,
And can digest as much. Make no compare
Between that love a woman can bear me
And that I owe Olivia.

Viola: Ay, but I know—

Orsino: What dost thou know?

Viola: Too well what love women to men may owe.
In faith, they are as true of heart as we.
My father had a daughter lov'd a man—
As it might be, perhaps, were I a woman,
I should your lordship.

Orsino: And what's her history?

→ CHALLENGE

1. How does Shakespeare have fun with the theme of appearance and reality in this scene?
2. Is Viola speaking honestly or dishonestly?
3. How does dramatic irony work here?

In the tragedies, the art of deception may be less blatant than donning a wig and false beard! However, it is likely to be just as obvious to the audience. In tragedies such as *Macbeth*, for example, the characters reveal their wicked intentions to the audience in soliloquies or in 'private' discussions with fellow conspirators. However, they play the role of honest friends and loyal subjects in the presence of their potential victims.

→ CHALLENGE

How is the idea of appearance and reality important in the play you are studying? Do characters use disguise or language to deceive others? What is the outcome of this deception?

Studying heritage poetry

There are 64 poems in the heritage poetry collection set by the exam board. Many students ask how many of these poems they should aim to read and study. You should read more poems than you write about in your final essay. In fact, the more you read, either informally or in detail, the more confident you are likely to become when writing about any poem. After all, literature is first and foremost about reading, and you need to show skill and experience in this in order to achieve the highest grades.

Avoid

Don't waste time adding in lots of details about the writer's life. You should always focus on the texts.

When you write your final piece of work for the assessment, you are best advised to write in detail about two or possibly three poems, while making reference to other texts or ideas that appear in the wider collection.

You may do some background reading around the poets or poems that you are studying, but it is very important that you do not lose track of your own 'voice' in your writing. You make an essay your own by being confident about what you write, and this confidence comes from the breadth and depth of your reading.

Themes in poetry

Themes in poetry need to be thought about a little more than most students appreciate. It is easy to follow a line of thinking that actually does not lead you to a deeper understanding of a particular poem. War is horrible, nature is beautiful, death is melancholy and so on. It is easy to make these generalized statements about themes without considering how the theme is presented in the specific poem you are reading. When writing about themes in poetry, you need to identify the writer's specific approach to, interest in and attitude towards the theme.

Themes can range from something concrete like people or places to something abstract like beliefs.

→ **CHALLENGE**

Look at the list of opening lines below. What themes can you identify within these lines? Do any of the themes relate to more than one poem?

Leisure

What is this life if, full of care,
We have no time to stand and stare?
W. H. Davies

Hawk Roosting

I sit in the top of the wood, my eyes closed
Ted Hughes

My Grandmother

She kept an antique shop – or it kept her.
Elizabeth Jennings

Sweet 18

You move before me with all the unknowing ease
of your age...
Sheenagh Pugh

You Will Be Hearing From Us Shortly

You feel adequate to the demands of this position?
U. A. Fanthorpe

Prayer Before Birth

I am not yet born; O hear me.
Louis MacNeice

Identifying the writer's attitude

Having some grip on the writer's attitude is crucial for a reader to have a good understanding of a poem, but it is not normally a case of 'spot the opinion' any more than one should 'spot the theme'. Expect attitudes to be subtle and complex at times. However, some ideas may be presented with great clarity and passion and you shouldn't ignore this. You need to combine sensitive reading skills with careful writing skills, to show your appreciation of the obvious points as well as the subtleties of language.

→ CHALLENGE

Select a poem from the collection that you haven't read. If you can, look through a few poems until you find one that relates to the theme you are studying. Read the poem and make some concise notes on the following:
- The voice and situation in the poem – who's speaking and what is the poem about?
- How does the poem link to the theme you are studying?
- What does the poet say about the theme; what attitudes and intentions are presented?

> **Avoid** ⚠
>
> Avoid making unrealistic claims about hidden meanings. Base your ideas on an overall understanding of the text.

Halfway between a theme and an attitude might be the notions of optimism and pessimism in poems. An 'optimistic' outlook is a positive or open-minded view, a 'pessimistic' outlook is negative or critical. There are definitely more poems with sober, serious endings than happy, cheerful ones, but writers are capable of provoking other complex thoughts and feelings in the reader too.

→ CHALLENGE

Explore the poetry collection for poems that are essentially optimistic in their view of life. Discuss what is inspiring or important about the poems you have identified.

Linking Shakespeare with heritage poetry

You can approach the 'linking' part of your final essay in different ways. However, you will probably write either a three-part or a two-part essay.

In a three-part essay, you would most likely write about your Shakespeare text first before moving on to write about the poetry collection. In the third part of your essay, you would then make comments that link the poetry with the Shakespeare play. If you take this approach, the third section will probably be the shortest part of the essay.

If you opt for a two-tier essay, you would write about the Shakespeare play first and then make links back to it as you write about the poetry in the second part of your essay. This can work very well, and can allow you to make some very effective links, but you need to make sure that you still explore the poems in detail.

→ CHALLENGE

Decide which approach you are going to take as part of your preparation for writing your final linked essay:
- Are you going to write a three-part essay where you write about the links between the texts at the end of the essay or are you going to link the texts in the second part of your essay?
- Be prepared to justify your choice with reference to your strengths. Use the **Upgrade** panel below to remind you of what you need to do to achieve the higher grades.

Upgrade

A* ↑	The response explores the Shakespeare play and the poetry with a similar level of detail. Links and points of comparison are clearly expressed, well organized and developed. The student is able to cross-reference between texts effectively.
A ↑	The response deals with both the Shakespeare play and the poetry in detail. Links are clearly expressed and relevant to the theme. The student is also able to use cross-reference to make points.
B	The response deals with both the Shakespeare play and the poetry. Links are relevant to the task and are explained.

Demonstrating high-level skills

The extracts that follow have been taken from a grade A* linked essay. This essay focuses on the theme of conflict in *Romeo & Juliet* and links this to relevant poems from the heritage poetry collection. This student is selective in her choice of poems, paying particular attention to 'Dulce et Decorum Est' by Wilfred Owen.

The extracts are taken from three different sections in the essay: the Shakespeare section, the heritage poems section and a third section that deals with the 'links' between the texts.

Read the extracts from the response and comments from the examiner, which show why this essay achieved high marks. The full assessment task is also given below.

- Examine the way Shakespeare presents the idea of the futility of conflict in *Romeo & Juliet*.
- How is the idea of the futility of conflict presented in poems in the collection? You can select poems to write about in detail but make references to others.
- Give your personal response to these texts, exploring the links between them.

Section 1: Writing about the Shakespeare text

The first two extracts are taken from the section of the essay that deals with the Shakespeare play.

Opening

A coherent overview. Every sentence offers some forward momentum in response to the question.

Conflict is the main theme in many pieces of writing and the conflict is often ended with a hero to resolve the situation. However, Romeo & Juliet is a tragedy which in itself introduces the idea of futility of conflict because you know the main characters and many others are going to die at some point in the play. Shakespeare set the play in 13th-century Italy, and at that time there were often pointless feuds between families, about power and status, so the Montague and Capulet families are typical of the time. They are two rich families feuding over something that nobody seems to remember, and the conflict results in the death of many people including the 'star cross'd lovers' Romeo and Juliet.

Good selection of detail. The student evaluates a scene that is important in connection with the theme.

Shakespeare introduces the theme of conflict straightaway in the play as Act 1 Scene 1 is a fight scene. The conversation between two Capulet servants shows how they would start a fight for no reason. Gregory says, 'The quarrel is between our masters, and us their men', which shows that they feel they have to fight to be loyal to their masters. They see the Montagues coming and Gregory says, 'Draw thy tool', even though there is no real reason to start a fight, which shows the futility of conflict...

Closing Paragraph

At the end of the play Capulet tells Lord Montague that he will build a statue for Romeo, to remember him by, and Montague replies, 'But, I can give thee more', meaning he can build an even better statue of Juliet. This gives you the feeling that, despite the shock and pain of losing their children, the feud is never going to end.

A memorable sentence, showing a confident interpretation of the text. This student writes with engagement and clarity.

Section 2: Writing about literary heritage poetry

The next two extracts are taken from the section of the essay that deals with the literary heritage poetry.

Opening

In the poem, 'Dulce et Decorum Est', Wilfred Owen presents the idea of futility of conflict in the First World War. Owen fought in the war so had first-hand experience of the conflict, and he died fighting in 1918, a year after he wrote this poem. He focuses on the Latin saying: 'Dulce et Decorum est/Pro patria mori', which means, 'it is sweet and fitting to die for one's country', and he says this is a lie.

His poem presents why this saying is 'the old lie' by showing the futility of conflict, based on a gas attack. Two other poems which share the idea of futility of conflict in the First World War are 'The Hero' by Siegfried Sassoon and 'The Conscript' by Wilfrid Gibson...

A well-constructed and emotive opening to the poetry section.

Some efficient use of background knowledge helps to highlight meaning in the text.

More could perhaps be said about the first poem before moving on.

Closing Paragraphs

'The Conscript' shows the futility of conflict by describing how each man was sent to his doom, without anybody seeming to care. 'The Hero' shows how each young man who died was thought of by his family as a strong, brave soldier because that is the glorified view of the war – how people want to believe it. But the truth, the reality of the war is that each man sacrificed everything for glory and no other reason, and the whole conflict was futile. It is so upsetting because all of these people lost their lives.

I think Wilfred Owen and the other two poets highlight the futility of conflict by showing all of the pain and suffering the soldiers had to go through. Despite this, nothing seems to change. This makes the audience realize just how futile the conflict was, because you are put in the soldier's shoes and realize the true horror of war.

A personal response is naturally integrated into the writing.

There is no over-reliance on technical terms here. This student writes successfully about meaning and with feeling.

Section 3: Links and personal response

The final extract is taken from the end of the essay, where the student discusses links between the texts.

Full Section

Although 'Romeo & Juliet' and 'Dulce et Decorum Est' are different forms, the first a play and the other a poem, they both leave the reader with a sense of sorrow about the futility of conflict.

There is perhaps some repetition here but the links are well realized and the student shows confidence moving from one text to another.

In 'Romeo & Juliet', Shakespeare presents the futility of conflict by focusing on a family feud over something trivial, in five acts, leading to the tragic death of the 'star cross'd lovers' Romeo and Juliet. On the other hand, Wilfred Owen focuses on the death of one soldier in a gas attack in the First World War. His poem highlights that the Latin saying 'Dulce et Decorum Est, Pro patria mori' is a lie and that the war was not as heroic as the government propaganda of the time made it out to be.

Perhaps nothing new in this final paragraph, but the student is able to sum up her argument effectively.

I think Shakespeare's play and Owen's poem are both upsetting pieces of writing which present the idea of the futility of conflict in a moving way. They both make the reader feel personally involved in different ways. The poem makes you realize just what soldiers in the war had to go through and that in reality, it was futile. Similarly, the play makes you wonder how something so trivial can lead to a family feud so tragic. Although they have different forms, structures and styles of language, they both leave a strong impact on the reader.

This is a highly committed piece of work that is clear-sighted, honest and very accomplished. The obvious thing to say is that, with the benefit of hindsight, a student working at this level might have pushed the boundaries a little more with the poetry, stretching the argument towards the protest element of Owen, Sassoon and others like Tennyson.

This student might have benefited from adopting a two-part essay structure rather than a three-part structure to avoid repetition in the later sections. However, despite some minor quibbles, this is a very strong piece of writing. The sky is the limit... but this essay is A*!

Final word

What makes a high-grade 'linked' response?

To reach the highest levels in this part of the course you need to show that you can write about Shakespeare and heritage poems as well as you can write about other texts. You need to show the same level of interest when exploring and questioning the attitudes and techniques demonstrated by the writer.

A top-grade student will have views about literature, displaying personal enjoyment and critical insight when writing about it. Grade A* answers will show a sensitivity to alternative interpretations and an integrated awareness of relevant historical contexts. Most strikingly, perhaps, A* students will show the ability to shape and develop a series of relevant points into a cogent **argument**.

When you write your linked essay, you should aim for quality over sheer quantity. You are advised to write around **2000 words**. Higher tier students typically write that amount, and more – too much more in some cases! Remember that you need to show control of your argument to reach the top grades, so you need to be selective and focused as well as showing a comprehensive understanding of the texts.

> ### Key words
>
> **Argument** – When writing an essay, you build an argument by linking individual points together to support your overall view.

Further task

In the following task, to end this chapter, you have an opportunity to deepen your understanding of the Shakespeare text you are studying and also to broaden your experience of working with the poetry collection by exploring both texts independently. In this task, you get a free choice in terms of which theme to focus on and indeed the freedom to identify a theme of your own.

Firstly, identify a list of themes that you feel are significant or interesting within the Shakespeare play you are studying. Discuss the themes as a class and then select one that you would like to explore further. Identify two poems from the poetry collection that deal with the theme in some way. Use these texts and the theme you have chosen to write an essay response to the task below.

Once you have completed your essay, use the **Upgrade** assessment criteria on the next page to assess the strengths and weaknesses of your essay.

- Select a theme of your choice. How does Shakespeare present this theme in the play that you are studying?
- How is the same theme explored in the poetry collection? Write about at least two poems in detail.
- Give your personal response to these texts, exploring the links between them.

Use the marking criteria below to assess your answer to the task on page 78. Decide how you could improve your work to help push your answer into the next grade band.

Critical response

1. Does the response show a consistent understanding of the texts and the ability to move comfortably from the specific to the general?
2. Does the response include perceptive and insightful comments about characters, relationships, attitudes and motives?
3. Does the response convey ideas persuasively and use well-selected evidence?

Language, structure, form

1. Does the response show appreciation of how writers use language to achieve specific effects?
2. Does the response evaluate the ways in which structure influences the meaning of the texts?

Links and comparisons

1. Does the response explore the Shakespeare play and the poetry with a similar level of detail?
2. Are links and points of comparison clearly expressed and well organized?

A*

Critical response

1. Does the response comment on the detail of the texts as well as the overall meaning of each text?
2. Does the response make relevant comments about characters, relationships, attitudes and motives?
3. Does the response convey ideas with precision?

Language, structure, form

1. Does the response show understanding of how writers use language to achieve effects?
2. Does the response make insightful points about how structure influences the meaning of the texts?

Links and comparisons

1. Does the response deal consistently with both the Shakespeare play and the poetry?
2. Are links clearly expressed?

A

Critical response

1. Does the response show comfortable understanding of each of the texts?
2. Does the response offer judgements about characters and relationships, attitudes and motives?
3. Does the response convey ideas clearly?

Language, structure, form

1. Does the response discuss how writers use language to achieve effects?
2. Does the response consider how structure influences the meaning of the texts?

Links and comparisons

1. Does the response deal evenly with both the Shakespeare play and the poetry?
2. Are links explained?

B

Acknowledgements

The publisher and author would like to thank the following for their permission to reproduce photographs and other copyright material.

p6: Malcolm Freeman/Alamy; **p7:** Urban Zone/Alamy; **p10-11:** Hank Frentz/Shutterstock; **p13:** Aleksander Bolbot/Shutterstock; p14: Brownstock/Alamy; **p17:** Jill Lang/Shutterstock; **p19:** Peter Lane/Alamy; **p21:** Terry Mathews/Alamy; **p28:** David Noton Photography/Alamy; **p31:** Christopher Holt/Alamy; **p32:** ImageState/Alamy; **p33:** Picture-Alliance/KPA Honorar & Belege; **p34:** AF archive/Alamy; **p37:** Paul Lindsay/Alamy; **p38:** Suzanne Tucker/Shutterstock; **p39:** AF archive/Alamy; **p41:** William Leaman/Alamy; **p42:** OUP/Image100; **p45:** Photos 12/Alamy; **p46:** AF archive/Alamy; **p50:** aberCPC/Alamy; **p52:** Paul Schlegelmann Photography; **p53:** Paul Lovelace/Rex Features; **p54:** Geraint Lewis/Alamy; **p55-57:** Photostage/Donald Cooper; **p58:** Joan Marcus; **p64:** Lebrecht Music and Arts Photo Library/Alamy; **p67-69:** Photostage/Donald Cooper; **p70:** Justin Russell; **p72l:** Papilio/Alamy; **p72r:** Andrew Woodward/Alamy; **p73:** incamerastock/Alamy.

The authors and publisher are grateful for permission to reprint the following copyright material:

Harold Brighouse: extracts from *Hobson's Choice* (Constable & Co, 1916/Heinemann 1992), reprinted by permission of the publishers, Constable & Robinson. *Billy Collins:* 'Introduction to Poetry' from *The Apple That Astonished Paris* (University of Arkansas Press, 2006), copyright © Billy Collins 1988, 1996, reprinted by permission of The Permissions Company, Inc., on behalf of the University of Arkansas Press, www.uapress.com. **Wendy Cope:** 'All-Purpose Poem for State Occasions' from *Making Cocoa for Kingsley Amis* (Faber, 1997), reprinted by permission of Faber & Faber Ltd. **Roddy Doyle:** extract from *Paddy Clarke Ha Ha Ha!* (Vintage, 2008), reprinted by permission of the Random House Group Ltd. **Robert Frost:** 'The Road Not Taken' from *The Poetry of Robert Frost* edited by Edward Conery Lathem (Cape 1971/Vintage, 2001), reprinted by permission of the Random House Group Ltd. **Tony Harrison:** 'Book Ends' from *Selected Poems* (Penguin, 2006), reprinted by permission of the author c/o Gordon Dickerson. **Nick Hornby:** extract from *About a Boy* (Penguin, 2002), copyright © Nick Hornby 1998, reprinted by permission of Penguin Books Ltd. **Ted Hughes:** 'Wind' from *Selected Poems 1957-1967* (Faber, 1972), reprinted by permission of Faber & Faber Ltd. **Philip Larkin:** 'Maiden Name' from *The Less Deceived* (Faber, 2011), reprinted by permission of Faber & Faber Ltd. **Leslie Adrienne Miller:** 'The Dead Send Their Gardener' from *The Resurrection Trade* (Graywolf, 2007), copyright © Leslie Adrienne Miller 2007, reprinted by permission of The Permissions Company Inc, on behalf of Graywolf Press, Minneapolis, Minnesota, www.graywolfpress.org. **Jean Nordhaus:** 'I Was Always Leaving', copyright © Jean Nordhaus 2008, first published in *The Gettysburg Review* Vol 21:4, Winter 2008, reprinted by permission of The Ohio State University Press. **J B Priestley:** extract from Act One of *An Inspector Calls* (Penguin Classics, 2001) originally published in 1944, copyright © J B Priestley 1944, 2001, reprinted by permission United Agents on behalf of The Estate of J B Priestley. **Willy Russell:** extracts from Act One of *Blood Brothers* (Methuen Drama, 2001), copyright © Willy Russell 1985, reprinted by permission of Methuen Drama, an imprint of Bloomsbury Publishing plc. **Owen Sheers:** 'Not Yet My Mother' from *The Blue Book* (Seren, 2000), reprinted by permission of the publishers; extract from *Resistance* (Faber, 2007), reprinted by permission of Faber & Faber Ltd. **Anne Stevenson:** 'Waving Goodbye' from *Stone Milk* (Bloodaxe, 2007), reprinted by permission of the publishers. **Mark Strand:** 'Eating Poetry', copyright © Mark Strand 1979, 1980, from *Selected Poems* (Carcanet, 1995) reprinted by permission of Carcanet Press Ltd and Alfred A Knopf, a division of Random House, Inc. **R S Thomas:** 'The Peasant' from *R S Thomas Selected Poems 1946-1968* (Bloodaxe, 1986), reprinted by permission of the publishers.

Although we have made every effort to trace and contact all copyright holders before publication this has not been possible in all cases. If notified, the publisher will rectify any errors or omissions at the earliest opportunity.